USING SECONDARY DATA IN MARKETING RESEARCH

USING SECONDARY DATA IN MARKETING RESEARCH

United States and Worldwide

GORDON L. PATZER

Q

QUORUM BOOKS
Westport, Connecticut • London

Library of Congress Cataloging-in-Publication Data

Patzer, Gordon L.
    Using secondary data in marketing research / by Gordon L. Patzer.
        p.   cm.
    Includes bibliographical references and index.
    ISBN 0–89930–961–5 (alk. paper)
    1. Marketing research.   2. Marketing—Information services.
    I. Title.
    HF5415.2.P38   1995
    658.8′3—dc20   94–40460

British Library Cataloguing in Publication Data is available.

Library of Congress Catalog Card Number: 94–40460
ISBN: 0–89930–961–5

First published in 1995

Quorum Books, 88 Post Road West, Westport, CT 06881
An imprint of Greenwood Publishing Group, Inc.

Printed in the United States of America

∞™

The paper used in this book complies with the
Permanent Paper Standard issued by the National
Information Standards Organization (Z39.48–1984).

10 9 8 7 6 5 4 3 2 1

Contents

Tables

Preface

The value of using secondary data for marketing research has been substantial throughout history, continues today, and promises to grow in the future. Its value is its capability to increase the efficiency and effectiveness of marketing research.

This book focuses on using secondary data for marketing research, in the present and the future, in the United States and around the world. It is divided into two major parts, with general qualities of secondary data presented first and specific sources of secondary data presented second.

Six chapters comprise Part I. To illustrate the importance of secondary data for effective marketing research to assist subsequent marketing decisions, a case study precedes Chapter 1. Chapter 1 is an introduction to secondary data within marketing research. Chapter 2 discusses the advantages and disadvantages of using secondary data, followed by considerations for evaluating secondary data in Chapter 3. Chapters 4 and 5 discuss two types of secondary data: internal and external, respectively. The last chapter in Part I, Chapter 6, pertains to locating secondary data in general. As such, it serves as a transition from the first part, which deals with the general qualities of secondary data, to the second part, which deals with specific sources of secondary data.

Part II is comprised of Chapters 7 through 11. It begins with a discussion about the importance of specific sources of secondary data, the increasing ease and computerization for using specific sources of secondary data in marketing research, and a cautionary note about the categorization of the specific information sources identified in Chapters 7 through 11. As in Part I, the beginning discussion of Part II includes a case study to introduce the importance of specific secondary data sources. Chapter 7 identifies sources of secondary data specific to marketing. Chapter 8 identifies global/worldwide information sources, while Chapter 9 deals with the American Census Data and pertinent reference guides. Chapter 10 presents categories of information sources that pertain to industries, corporate directories, and investments/finances. The final chapter, Chapter 11, identifies sources for business information that are not specific to marketing. It also identifies secondary data sources that are rather general and dissimilar, but can be beneficial to obtaining secondary data to assist relevant marketing decision making.

PART I

GENERAL QUALITIES OF SECONDARY DATA

CASE STUDY

Several years earlier, the chief executives at Guinness Brewing Company had begun their decision process concerning whether to expand operations into the Hong Kong market.[1] The company, with headquarters in Dublin, Ireland, was already marketing its flagship product in over a hundred countries. Its flagship product, Guinness Beer, is accurately categorized as a stout or ale. Such a dark brown, as to be almost black in color, Guinness Stout contrasts with the light-colored American beers, which are categorized in the British Isles and many other parts of the world as lagers.

Hoping to avoid reaching an incorrect decision, Guinness Brewing wanted marketing research information to assist their decision making. Their list of questions was long. For example, they wanted to know:

How many people live in Hong Kong?

What is their age distribution?

What is their income?

What is their education?

Where are the people located in the city and country?

What are the demographic characteristics of people by areas within the city and country?

How do the people live in terms of housing?

How much beer is consumed, in total and per capita?

What type of beer is preferred?

What brands currently exist?

What are the market shares of the different brands?

How is beer purchased in Hong Kong? For example, what portion of the beer market is comprised of single servings in restaurants (and what kind of restaurants) and drinking establishments (such as bars, nightclubs, and hotel lounges) and what portion of the beer market is comprised of multiple packs (and what size packs, since the soft drinks sold at grocery stores are sold only as single cans or in packs of eight).

How many tourists visit Hong Kong each year?

How much beer do these tourists consume?

Much, but not all, of this information already existed in the form of secondary data. For example, from the secondary data it was determined that Hong Kong had a population of about 5.7 million people in an area of about 400 square miles, and is on the doorstep of China with a population of well over 1 billion people. While over forty brands of beer are marketed in Hong Kong, San Miguel has an overwhelming market share of approximately 80 percent. It was also determined from secondary data that per capita beer consumption was low at about 27.1 liters per year, and that income was around HK $9,000 per month. The education of most residents did not include "tertiary" school.

The Guinness Brewing company was confronted with both the benefits and detriments of using secondary data. It was beneficial that, since much of the desired information already had been gathered, it could be obtained with minimum expenditures in time and money.

Typically, however, detriments were also present. First, unlike the government system in the United States, which reports substantial census information according to zip code, or in England and Ireland, where an analogous system utilizes postal codes, Hong Kong had no such mail or postal delivery system. Second, much of the data or information had been collected several years earlier, and some even as much as eight to ten years earlier. Third, it seemed possibly that some of the more positive information was too optimistic (and may have been prepared by city promoters hoping to attract industry). Fourth, some critical information was reported only in Chinese (Cantonese, to be exact) rather than English. Fifth, much of the information that was available had to be translated or converted. For example, per capita beer consumption had to be converted from liters to pints and barrels, the Hong Kong dollar had to be translated into Irish pounds (or punts), and the education system referred to as tertiary school had to be interpreted in terms of primary, secondary, college, and university education levels.

The conclusion was that these secondary data substantially helped the Guinness Brewing executives make their decision about expanding into the Hong Kong market. The availability of these secondary data saved time and money and also helped form the foundation and context for conducting a more efficient and effective marketing research project pertaining to the potential of Guinness Beer in Hong Kong. However, these data were not perfect. Much of the data were not relevant because of their age and how they were reported, while other data were difficult to meaningfully convert into the home country's system in Ireland.

NOTE

1. This example is based on the author's own experience and conversations with beer industry executives during 1992 and 1993 when he lived in Dublin, Ireland, and Hong Kong.

1

Introduction to Secondary Data

Marketing research routinely utilizes many types of data and information. The single most prevalent type is data and other pieces of information that were first collected for another purpose. When such data are used in a particular marketing research project, this use is then the second use and the data are correspondingly referred to as *secondary data*.[1] The title does not signify secondary importance, minor value, or inferior quality. These data are collected and analyzed first, before primary data, in most marketing research projects.

Primary data are data, or other pieces of information, collected for the purpose of the current marketing research project. Generally, marketing research relies on secondary data to complement primary data. However, secondary data are being used increasingly as the sole information to assist users of marketing research in their decision making. Even if existing information does not address exactly the questions posed by a current marketing research project, information likely exists for similar questions, which eliminates or at least reduces the need for primary data.

Consider the marketing decisions by Leading Edge Computers, headquartered in Korea, as the firm questioned its market potential among American manufacturers in the ten most populated states. Information was needed about the major types of manufacturers, along with their size, number, and exact locations. Subsequent research based solely on secondary data provided this information. For example, most states publish directories of manufacturers, their size (sales, number of employees, number of factories, square footage, etc.), location, names of principal executives, contact information, and much more.

The most frequent application of secondary data in marketing research is to gain familiarity and to establish a context in which primary data are collected, analyzed, and reported, the problem is defined, and the research is designed. This application is a *literature search*—an examination of existing material, searching for information pertinent to the current marketing research project. Materials are typically scholarly journals, magazines, books, newspapers, and company records (accessed through computer data bases).

Secondary data can provide information about techniques and procedures for conducting marketing research. For example, these data can help determine language for communicating with the research sample members (i.e., vocabulary and grammar to use and not to use when attempting to communicate with research participants such as survey respondents or subjects in an experiment, which might be individuals, organizations, or other entities), questions and topics to avoid, problems likely to be encountered, and statistical techniques to employ.

Two major types of secondary data are internal secondary data and external secondary data. Within each of these categorizations there are many considerations which range from creating internal secondary data to accessing external secondary data.

Secondary data is a potentially misleading term for people not experienced with marketing research. For example, it is misleading to think of secondary data as being of second importance, minor importance, inferior value, or in any way not necessary. Their worth, like that of all data, depends instead on the marketing research project. However, it is reasonable to conclude that secondary data play a significant role in almost all marketing research projects. Another misconception is to think of secondary data as coming second in a sequence. The sequential order is just the opposite: secondary data typically are collected and analyzed first, before primary data.

MARKETING RESEARCH PROCESS

Rarely does a marketing research project rely *solely* on secondary data. At the same time, rarely does a marketing research project not rely on secondary data at all. Three stages of the marketing research process are especially pertinent to the use of secondary data: problem definition, research design, and report presentation. Within these stages, the use of secondary information pertains to project information, foundation and context, and techniques and tools.

Project Information

Secondary data generally do not substitute for, or compete with, primary data. Rather, they are complementary. At the same time, there are some marketing situations in which secondary data are the only data required to assist users of marketing research in their decision making. Users of marketing research are confronted with recurring decisions. It is therefore likely that helpful secondary information will exist.

Foundation and Context

The most frequent application of secondary data in marketing research is not as sole project information, but as groundwork to establish a foundation and context. On this foundation and in this context, primary data are collected, analyzed, and reported. The groundwork is laid in the form of a *literature search*.

A *literature search* is a search among existing material for information pertinent to the current marketing research project. It is often an aspect of exploratory research, through which marketing researchers gain familiarity with the topic of their current marketing research project. Typical materials utilized in a literature search are computer data bases, books, magazines, scholarly journals, newspapers, and company records.

Secondary data obtained via computerized literature searches are helpful to define the problem, design the research, analyze the data, and discuss the results. For example, secondary data help in the following ways:

> Problem definition—Refine, and even redirect, objectives, questions, and information to be addressed by a marketing research project.

> Research design—Properly word and order questions, which includes avoiding words that might be misunderstood or offensive. Secondary data eliminate questions if the answers are already known, which is always desirable since shorter questionnaires are completed with greater accuracy and at a higher rate than longer questionnaires.

> Data analysis—Identify the proper statistical techniques.

> Discussion of results and report presentation—Provide meaning to data by explaining the findings from a current marketing research project within the context of findings from other studies.

Consider a situation in which marketing executives at the Folger's Coffee Company were concerned about a downturn in sales of their flagship brand. At the problem definition stage, the focus was on why people in general were drinking less Folger's Coffee at present compared to one year ago. The corresponding research design was planned up to the point at which a literature search discovered that coffee consumption was not the same across age groups. It was actually increasing among people aged fifty-five to sixty-five years of age, while decreasing dramatically among people under twenty-five years of age. The problem definition and research design were revised, accordingly, based on this information. Now the problem definition and research design were refocused on: (1) why people aged eighteen to twenty-five years of age were drinking less coffee than one year ago, and (2) coffee consumption in general, rather than consumption of Folger's in particular.

Techniques and Tools

In addition to foundation and context, secondary data provide information about techniques and tools to utilize. The information in this regard can help to determine proper language and terminology with which to communicate with the sample units (i.e., research participants such as survey respondents or subjects in an experiment, which might be individuals, organizations, or other entities), questions and topics that should be avoided, and problems likely to be encountered.

NOTE

1. *Secondary information* is used synonymously with *secondary data* and, in practice, the two terms are used interchangeably.

2

Advantages and Disadvantages of Secondary Data

The adage that there is no need to reinvent the wheel is pertinent to the role of secondary data within marketing research. Specifically, it is not necessary for marketing researchers to wait for (or pay for) a research project to collect primary data if the desired information already exists. Therefore, the two major advantages of secondary data over primary data are:

1. Savings in time, and

2. Monetary savings.

Tables 2.1 and 2.2, respectively, identify reasons that underlie the time and money savings. They include experience factors (also known as learning curves), economies of scale, multiple buyers, government subsidies, association dues, market forces, and prices that reflect costs. Furthermore, even when primary data are collected in addition to secondary data, the secondary data enhance the efficiency and effectiveness of collecting, analyzing, and reporting of the primary data.

These two advantages are demonstrated well by the situation confronted by the Guinness Brewing company in the opening case study example. For a minimum expenditure of time and money, the

Table 2.1
Secondary Data Saves Time

The time saved for individual users of secondary data is
obvious, since they need only locate a provider of the data rather
than perform the initial research themselves. However, even
though, for secondary data to exist, someone must perform
marketing research, the total time expended is still less than if
individual users performed the research themselves. There are
two reasons:

1. The experience factor or learning curve regarding
    the larger quantity of such research performed by an
    individual or organization lowers the total time
    required.

2. Economies of scale are realized because research
    efforts are not duplicated. Having one source
    initially collect and process the data, which an
    infinite number of users can then obtain, is more
    efficient in terms of time than having each of the
    users individually collect and process the data for
    themselves.

This total time savings is more prominent when you realize that
some research activities are sequential and dependent on other
efforts and people. For example, the speed with which data
collection forms are printed, questionnaires completed, and
mailed materials returned by respondents, is largely out of the
control of researchers. Therefore, even if a marketing research
project is possible to complete in 200 work hours, these work
hours must be spread over a longer period of time than simply
five 40-hour work weeks.

Table 2.2
Secondary Data Saves Money for Individual Researchers

Researchers save money when obtaining secondary data because of five reasons:

1. MULTIPLE BUYERS

   Charges to pay costs incurred by a provider of secondary data are shared among multiple users.

2. GOVERNMENT SUBSIDIES

   Government taxes from general revenue sources underwrite the generating of government-sponsored information.

3. ASSOCIATION DUES

   Membership dues underwrite trade association information.

4. MARKET FORCES

   Providers of secondary data compete among themselves to provide users with the best price.

5. PRICE REFLECTS COST

   The cost of secondary data is lower than that of performing the research individually due to experience factors and economies of scale associated with performing larger quantities of respective research. Cost is also lower due to work that may have been performed at an earlier time—often years earlier—when wage rates may have been lower and the provider may have had fewer production costs, work pressures, and time deadlines.

---

company received information to assist their decision about expanding into the Hong Kong market. It included desired information about the population of Hong Kong, their education and income, and per capita beer consumption. It even included information about the marketplace, with its forty brands, and the major competitor: the San Miguel Beer Company with over 80 percent of the market share.

Furthermore, while secondary data rarely answers all the questions of a marketing research project, the data usually provide some answers. A subsequent value is that efforts to collect primary data can be more focused. Rather than rediscover information that already exists, questions that are unnecessary to answer with primary data are identified in advance. An example is the opening case study example where secondary information for Guinness Brewing provided context in which to obtain focused primary data about the major competitor, the San Miguel Beer Company.

As well as advantages, secondary data possess three major disadvantages:

1. Recency, which is less than desired;

2. Relevance, which is less than ideal for questions posed by the current research; and

3. Accuracy, which is not known.

The disadvantages of secondary data exist because researchers for a current marketing research project lack direct control of the date, type, and procedure for collecting and recording the data. As a result, some secondary data may be of little or no value, or even negative value if they misinform. Researchers do have indirect control, limited largely to deciding whether or not to use the data, or whether to use them with qualifications. However, since the already large amount of secondary data continually grows and changes, the time, money, and effort required to obtain desired data are often greater than anticipated.

These disadvantages were illustrated well by the problems encountered when the Guinness Brewing Company was deciding about entering the Hong Kong beer market. The company encountered disadvantages that are not untypical for secondary data, including complications inherent in the international marketplace. For example, the Guinness Brewing Company had to contend with the age of the

data, unfamiliar reporting categories, language and measurement differences, and questions about accuracy, all which had to be over-come
to ensure the information was meaningful for assisting decisions by
company executives in a distant country.

ELABORATION OF THE ADVANTAGES

The chief advantages of secondary data, over primary data, are
savings in time and money.

Time Savings

Whoever performs marketing research activities, and whenever
they are performed, time is required to plan and conduct them.
Additional time for waiting is also required since some activities are
sequential and dependent on the efforts and time commitments of
other people and activities.

With secondary data, the information already exists. Someone has
performed the necessary activities earlier for either another purpose
or another marketing research project. The time necessary to complete
these activities was expended by someone else unrelated to the current
marketing research project. Rather than going through the data
collection steps, marketing researchers can simply access material
such as computer data bases, books, magazines, scholarly journals,
newspapers, and company records. The consequence is that once a
user approves a marketing research project, the respective information
(if it exists in the form of secondary data) will be available in less
time than is possible (or practical) with primary data.

Money Savings

Whoever conducts them and whenever marketing research
activities are performed, there are financial costs required to plan and
conduct them. There is no free lunch, so to speak. Just as with the
required activities and required amounts of time, someone must pay
the financial costs. These costs can be shifted through using secondary
data (although they cannot be eliminated). As a result, a large amount

of the cost, and at times practically the entire cost, is shifted away from the marketing researchers involved with the current project, and therefore away from those who use this marketing research to assist their decision making. The consequence is that secondary data are generally much less expensive than primary information.

Who pays the original cost for secondary data if the costs charged to a current marketing research project are either greatly reduced or even waived completely? To begin, the costs associated with secondary data might be less than the costs associated with the same data collected at the time of a current marketing research project. In addition to the impact of time periods on cost for secondary data, the cost is also lower because payment can come from at least different three sources: government taxes, association dues, and shared charges.

Time Periods

While not a source for paying the cost of producing secondary data, time periods represent an important related aspect. Depending on the time period in which the secondary data are produced, the costs may be lessened. In turn, these lower costs will be reflected in the lower charges for a current marketing research project.

Secondary data are collected in a time period earlier than the current marketing research project. Therefore, fewer time pressures in the form of time deadlines—with correspondingly lower production costs—are likely to be involved. Moreover, in economic times of relatively high inflation, an earlier time period may be a period of lower prices and costs.

Government Taxes

Government taxes underwrite government-sponsored information. There is a wealth of such information, and it is in no means limited to the valuable census data produced by the American government. As well as the examples of government information identified in this book, the reader is referred to an enlightening list of information provided by the American government that is identified in a book by Matthew Lesko and titled *Lesko's Info-Power Sourcebook*.[1] The actual costs of producing these data originally are not charged to a current marketing research project because such government-sponsored information is paid by taxes, usually from general revenue sources.

Association Dues

Association dues underwrite trade association information. Almost every industry has a trade association that assesses membership dues. Among the uses of these dues are specialized industry studies. People interested in a particular industry can usually obtain such studies either at no cost or for a relatively nominal fee.

Shared Charges

Shared charges refer to secondary data obtained from business organizations that sell secondary information. Even in these situations, secondary information is less costly because the charges are spread over a number of marketing research projects. In other words, those for whom marketing research projects are conducted are charged a prorated fee. Collectively, the charges pay the cost of producing the secondary data as well as provide the business organization with a profit for its efforts.

Marketing Research Process

Activities necessary to conduct a marketing research project must be performed by someone. The activities, along with the required money and time, can be shifted but not eliminated. For marketing researchers and users of marketing research, an advantage of using secondary information is that numerous costly activities in the marketing research process are avoided. These activities are those normally associated with primary data collection and include the following:

Sample—selecting units (such as people, households, organizations, etc.) from whom to gain information, and then contacting them.

Data Collection—designing data collection forms, printing them, interacting with sample units to administer the forms or questionnaires, and so on.

Data Analysis—processing the collected data, preparing them (e.g., cleaning the data to remove apparent mistakes and then coding the data in a computer compatible format), transferring them to computer files, tabulating them, and so forth.

Fieldwork—arranging procedures for selecting, supervising, and compensating personnel, and so on.

Marketing researchers involved with a current research project, as well as the users of the marketing research, can save time and money by avoiding these activities through use of secondary data.

Efficiency and Effectiveness

Advantages of using secondary data translate into substantial benefits of efficiency and effectiveness. While secondary data rarely answer all the questions of a marketing research project, they usually provide some answers. A subsequent value is that efforts to collect primary data can be more focused. Rather than rediscover information that is already known, questions that are unnecessary to answer with primary data are identified in advance.

Consider the Sony Corporation's decision to market a digital audio tape (DAT) system. A reasonable strategy is to first enter American cities with minimum metropolitan populations of 250,000 people and a specified minimum number of households having per capita household incomes of at least $35,000 and at least one male resident. If Sony commissioned a marketing research project to determine this information using primary data, the cost in time and money would be prohibitive.

Sony, however, can identify cities meeting these criteria quickly and inexpensively with secondary data. This information can be obtained through any one of several secondary data sources, such as American government census data, the "Survey of Buying Power" that is a series of statistics published regularly in the *Sales and Marketing Management* magazine, and companies specializing in demographic data. At this point, Sony might be interested about awareness among its target market about the superior sound of DAT. To obtain this information it will be necessary to collect primary data. However, because secondary data exist for a portion of Sony's questions, subsequent research can zero in more effectively and efficiently on primary data deemed necessary for its marketing strategy. The alternative is to become inefficiently and unnecessarily bogged down obtaining primary data that already exists.

ELABORATION OF THE DISADVANTAGES

Few things in life are perfect, and secondary data are no exception. While the cost of this information is low, in the worst-case scenario, its value may be as low as to have a zero or even negative value. The reason for this potentially low value is because there are disadvantages as well as advantages in using secondary data. The two major disadvantages pertain to relevance and accuracy.

Lack of relevance and lack of accuracy in marketing research are associated with using secondary data rather than primary data. These disadvantages exist regardless of whether a marketing research project includes primary data. As a result, at times, not only may secondary data be of little or no assistance to a user of marketing research, they can actually be detrimental.

Underlying both these disadvantages is a lack of control. People associated with a current marketing research project have no direct control over the original, now secondary, data. Thus, they are unable to exert control over either the type of data (relevance) or the way in which the data were collected (accuracy). Their only control is indirect, limited to deciding whether or not to use the data, or whether to use the data with qualifications.

RELEVANCE

Secondary data, by definition, exist for a purpose other than the one. A consequent is that secondary data cannot be expected to be as relevant to a current marketing research project as primary data. A dimension of this lack of relevancy is that secondary data are often available in a more general form or a different format than desired for a current marketing research project.

The relevance of secondary data is a judgment made both by marketing researchers involved with the current research project and by those who use that research information to assist their decision making. The relevance of secondary data is not a yes-no judgment but instead spans a continuum ranging from highly relevant to the current marketing research project to not at all relevant. Even when the secondary data are judged to be highly relevant, they rarely provide the precise marketing research information desired by the user. Therefore, rather than sufficing as primary data, secondary data at the highly relevant end of the continuum are most useful in establishing the foundation and context for collecting and analyzing primary data. At the opposing end of the continuum, secondary data are not at all relevant and are likely to actually be a detriment if used in decision making. Secondary data between these two extremes are the most common in marketing research. These data are of varying value and must be used cautiously as their relevance permits.

Judgment about the relevance of secondary data is not necessarily a judgment about the information's inherent quality. Since the data were collected for another purpose, the judgment is mostly about their application, fit, or suitability for the information needs of the current marketing research project. Typical considerations affecting the relevance of secondary data involve age of data, terms of data, and units of data.

Age of Data

Older data are generally not as pertinent to most marketing decisions as newer data. While many principles of marketing strategy remain relatively constant, there are rapid changes in the dynamic environments in which marketing functions. A market's demographics change regularly, as do the preferences, beliefs, and attitudes of people within these markets.

The age factor of secondary data is somewhat situational. Pieces of information, like most things in life, age at different rates. Marketing research information about a basic consumer behavior might still remain current after ten years, while similar information about a fad product might become outdated after a few weeks. Therefore, the relevance of the age of secondary depends on the type of marketing decision confronted by the user.

Secondary data, by definition, were collected at an earlier time than the time of the current marketing research project. These differences in time can lower the relevance of the information, but in some situations, this difference is unavoidable. When comprehensive population data are desired, the time to collect and process the information must be taken into account. If these time frames are not acceptable for the marketing decision at hand, other information must be sought.

Government census information is valuable for marketing decision makers. However, given its volume and cost, even under the best of conditions it takes time for governments to provide this information. For example, currently, in the mid-1990s the United States has about 260 million people and conducts a population census every ten years. It then takes the American government up to three years, and in some situations even more time, to release its official population census information.

For a more extreme case, consider the situation of a marketing executive who is confronted with a decision pertaining to census data about China. The country has over four times as many people as the United States, only a fraction of the resources, and few of the latest technological means for conducting a census. As a consequence, China is believed to now have over 1.2 billion people, but it does not conduct a population census on a set time table. For example, it was twenty-nine years before the most recent population census was conducted in China (1982). Related, its first Similarly, that nation's first industrial census was not conducted until 1986.

Categories of Data

Categories and terms for data often vary. People who conduct the original data collection frequently categorize the data differently then is desired for the current marketing research project. This difference is especially problematic with information about populations. While the information may be similar, it may not be directly comparable.

Consider a comparison of standard government census data and television viewing data, such as provided by the Arbitron company. Arbitron provides information about television viewing audiences in the over two hundred television (broadcasting) station markets in the

United States. The information is relevant for many marketing decisions, but its relevance is lowered for some marketing research projects because of differences between marketing executives who need dissimilar categorizations. For example, Arbitron reports its information according to *area of dominant influence* (ADI). Area of dominant influence is the geographical area in which a television station receives the most viewers. Unfortunately, this geographical area is not compatible with areas described in government population census data, which are also of interest to marketing executives. The government's reporting of information, according to geographical area, categorizes the information according to *metropolitan statistical area* (MSA)—an urban area in which at least 50,000 people live, and that is separate economically and socially from other urban areas.

Even when the overall market or population areas are the same, specific aspects of the data are frequently categorized differently. For example, consider demographic information about income, education, and ethnicity.

Income

Some secondary data presents income in terms of an individual respondent (such as the head of household). That is of little relevance to a current marketing research project interested in total income categorized according to households. Similarly, one set of data might define income in terms of annual employment compensation while the needs of a current project may be for income that includes interest and investments, as well as employment compensation.

Another problem with using secondary data for income involves the numerical categories. A current marketing research project might be interested in the percentages of people in a particular market whose income is less than $25,000; $25,001 to $50,000; and more than $50,000. However, the secondary data available for that market might be reported in increments of $10,000, beginning at $20,000 (less than $20,000; $20,001 to $30,000; $30,001 to $40,000; etc.).

Education

A current marketing research project might need education information in categories such as completion of: high school, two-year college program, four-year college diploma, master's degree, and Ph.D. degree. However, the available secondary data might only present education information in categories designated as high school, college, and postgraduate study.

The relevance of secondary information about education is especially troublesome when marketing research information is needed about different countries. Names of degrees, as well as respective time requirements and courses of study, vary widely between countries. For example, a four-year college degree in the United States is a bachelor's, but in a European country such as France, it is a *maitrise*. Even after getting around the difficulty of the language translation (*maitrise* translates into master's), the time involved is not comparable to earning the American degrees. Specifically, a French *maitrise* is more than an American bachelor's degree and less than an American master's degree. Such difficulties occur around the world. For example, a bachelor's degree earned in a location like Hong Kong or England is a three-year degree, but in Scotland, a bachelor's degree is a four-year degree.

Ethnicity

A current marketing research project might need ethnicity information in categories such as Puerto Rican, Cuban, and Mexican-American, but available secondary data may present this information as one total category designated Hispanic or Latino. Secondary data might categorize people of Korean, Japanese, Philippine, Chinese, and Indian descent into one category designated Asian. Similarly, secondary data might use the category white or Caucasian, while a current marketing research project might need information categorized according to German, English, French, and Italian heritages.

Further complicating the situation is the fact that changes in ethnicity categories occur over time. Secondary data dealing with ethnicity in the United States has long used the designation of black, but in the early 1990s, designations such as Afro-American and then, later, African-American emerged. Thus, a current marketing research project needing information about black Americans might have difficulty with data classifying individuals as African-Americans. For example, one problem is that not all people living in or coming from

Africa are black. There are many white people born in African countries, and yet the African-American designation for secondary data does not differentiate between black African-Americans and white African-Americans. Consider, for example, the 1992 Miss Universe contest winner, Michelle McLean, who was born and raised in Namibia and is white.

Even without changes in terminology, racial and ethnic designations pose problems for those who perform marketing research and for those who utilize such secondary data. For example, consider the common practice of categorizing the great diversity of people in the United States into a few broad categories. The problem is that each of these categories is commonly then composed of people who are very dissimilar in many ways related to marketing, consumer behavior, and otherwise. An example of this categorization of secondary data is presented in Table 2.3.

Units of Data

Units of data provide another difficulty when using secondary data in current marketing research projects. First, different units are used to define terms. Consider a research project focusing on the size of certain businesses. The current project might be interested in size as defined by square footage. However, the most relevant secondary data might define size in terms of number of employees, sales revenue, or even amount of profit.

Second, as with ethnicity designations, changes occur in units of data. The United States is slowly moving from use of the American units of measurement (feet, pounds, etc.) to metric units (meters, kilograms, etc.). Thus, secondary information from the past and present will in the future represent older information that is not calculated in the units desired by the then-current marketing research projects.

Third, the problems involved with using units of data within a country is magnified when comparisons are made between countries. The United States is one of the few countries in the world in which the metric system is not standard. Therefore, an American marketing executive looking at opportunities elsewhere in the world must convert the metric measurement system into the American measurement

Table 2.3
Common Categories of Race and Ethnicity

When secondary data are reported in the United States, the diversity of people from whom the data are collected are often placed into a relatively few broad categories. The problem for marketing research is that within each of these categories there is great variation between the peoples represented. Despite their great diversity, secondary data are commonly reported as follows.

Asian—All people of the Far East, Southeast Asia, Pacific Islands, and the Indian subcontinent. These people include everyone with such origins as Cambodian, Chinese, Filipino, Guamanian/Chamorran, Hawaiian, Indian, Japanese, Korean, Malaysian, Samoan, Thai, and Vietnamese.

Black—All people descended from black racial groups of Africa (but not of Hispanic origin).

Hispanic—All people of Spanish, Latin-American, and Latino culture or origin, regardless of race. These people include everyone with such origins as Cuban, Mexican-American/Chicano, and Puerto Rican.

Native American—All people originally from North America with cultural identification maintained through tribal affiliation or communication recognitions. These people include everyone with such origins as American Indians of all tribes and nations (Cherokee, Hopi, Seminole, Sioux, etc.) and Alaskan natives (Aleut, Eskimo, Haida, etc.).

White—All people originally from Europe, North Africa, and the Middle East (but not of Hispanic origin). These people include everyone with such origins as European (British, French, German, Italian, Polish, Russian, Swiss, etc.), Middle Eastern (Israeli, Lebanese, Saudi Arabian, Iranian, Iraqi, Kuwaiti, etc.), and North African.

system. Likewise, marketing executives elsewhere in the world who are interested in making use of the large amount of secondary data in and about the United States must convert the American measurement system into the metric system.

Marketing research involving international information is always complicated by differences in units. Every country has its own currency, and even when the same unit name is used, the numerical value differs. For example, the dollar ($) is the currency designation in the United States, Canada, and Hong Kong. However, considering the American dollar as the standard for a moment, 1 American dollar equals about 1.2 Canadian dollars and about 7.4 Hong Kong dollars. In fact the dollar (with different values in each country), is also the official local currency in at least fifteen other countries: Australia, Bahamas, Barbados, Belize, Canada, East Caribbean, Fiji, Guyana, Hong Kong, Jamaica, Liberia, New Zealand, Singapore, Solomon Islands, and Taiwan.

Difficulties of using secondary data in marketing research are further complicated by international nuances and changes. For example, China has 2 currencies: Renminbi (RMB) and Foreign Exchange Currency (FEC). The Commonwealth of Independent States (CIS)[2] has relatively recently, and dramatically, changed the value of its country's currency (the ruble) by joining the International Monetary System (IMF). All the countries of the European Economic Community (EEC) are scheduled to discontinue their separate currencies in 1996 (per the Maastricht Treaty). The consequence will be a single currency replacing each of the respective currencies identified in Table 2.4. The one currency planned to replace the twelve separate currencies of the EEC nations is the European Currency Unit (ECU).

ACCURACY

Lack of accuracy of secondary data is a more serious disadvantage for marketing research than is lack of relevance. The reason is that the likelihood is higher for a user of marketing research to make a decision based on secondary data that are inaccurate than on those that are irrelevant. Relevance or suitability can be more readily determined by the people associated with a current marketing research project, who can then omit or restrict the application of secondary data to a

Table 2.4
Countries of the European Economic Community and Their
Respective Currencies (1992)

As of 1992, the European Economic Community (EEC) was comprised of twelve core nations that represent 320 million people. These countries and their respective currencies are:

Belgium	Franc (Belgian franc: BF)
Denmark	Krone (Danish krone: DKr)
France	Franc (French franc: FF)
Germany	Mark (German mark: DM)
Greece	Drachma (Greek drachma: Dr)
Ireland	Pound (Irish pound: Ir)
Italy	Lire (Italian lira: ILir)
Luxembourg	Franc (Lux franc: F)
Netherlands	Florin or gilder (Dutch florin or Dutch guilder: fl)
Portugal	Escudo (Portuguese escudo: Esu)
Spain	Peseta (Spanish ptas: Ptas)
United Kingdom	Pound (British sterling: Sterling)

Although it is seldom acknowledged, within the United Kingdom there are actually two pounds: the British pound, issued by the Bank of England, and the Scottish pound, issued by the Bank of Scotland.

marketing decision if they appear not to fit the current project.

As with irrelevant data, secondary data that appear inaccurate can be omitted or restricted. However, the accuracy of secondary data cannot be readily or so assuredly determined as the relevance by the people associated with a current marketing research project. A reason is that inaccurate data are less apparent then irrelevant data. The consequence is that a false assumption of accuracy of secondary data for a current marketing research project is more likely to occur than a false assumption of relevance.

Inaccurate secondary data can be either accidental or intentional. Inaccuracies that are accidental occur at almost any stage of the process, from planning to reporting the data. Since one type of secondary data is collected earlier as primary data, all the problems associated with primary data also apply. These problems might be as elementary as a simple typographical error in numbers when they were recorded.

However, accidental inaccuracies may be more subtle. They might involve any one (or more) of the many activities involved in sampling, data collection, data analysis, and report presentation. Accidental inaccuracies are especially likely in large research efforts such as a national census. They may be especially subtle and serious because the current user of the data may be unable to determine how, precisely, each of the important activities was conducted.

Unfortunately, there are also intentional inaccuracies. Research conducted by another person may be slanted in a way that supports a particular interest. Not only do individuals and research organizations occasionally slant, distort, or even mis-report research findings, but governments (local and foreign) may also do so in an attempt to put the best face on their situation when marketing decisions are made about possible expansions into the government's area. Therefore, it is conceivable that governments concerned about their image and political positions might intentionally distort both unfavorable and favorable information to their advantage.

Counteractions

People associated with a current marketing research project are not helpless in regard to issues of determining secondary data accuracy. Their decisions can be to assume accuracy and use the data, assume some inaccuracy and use the data with qualifications, or assume unacceptable inaccuracy and avoid using the data. The next chapter discusses various direct actions that can be taken to evaluate secondary data.

NOTES

1. Matthew Lesko, *Lesko's Info-Power Sourcebook* (Kensington, MD: Information U.S.A., 1990).

2. Formerly the Union of Soviet Socialist Republics (USSR).

3

Evaluating Secondary Data

Secondary data should not be accepted automatically at face value. As noted in the prior chapter, potential complications to consider include: age of data, categories of data, units of data, and accuracy of data. The first three—age, categories, and units—are frequently acknowledged areas that carry disadvantages for secondary data.

DISADVANTAGES

Appearances can be deceiving, since better alternatives do not always exist for secondary data that appear to possess a disadvantage or weakness. For example, although relevance is generally greater for newer data than older data, age is situational and dependent on the particular marketing research project. Information about a basic consumer behavior might remain applicable after many years, while similar information about a fad product might be outdated after a few weeks.

Also, less than immediate data are inevitable in some situations. Consider the time necessary for governments to process the huge volume associated with comprehensive population data. In the United States the government takes up to three years, and more in some situations, to release its official population census, which is collected every ten years. More extreme, consider marketing executives confronted with a decision pertaining to population census data about China, with a population about five times greater than the United States combined with a fraction of the resources and technologies to conduct a census.

At the same time, secondary data have little, if any, relevance when the categories and units are not compatible with the needs of a current marketing research project. For example, income categorized according to an individual (e.g., the head of household or the individual respondent to a questionnaire) has little relevance for a research project that requires income categorized according to total household. Similarly, secondary data that define income in terms of annual employment compensation conflicts with a project that requires income inclusive of interest, investment returns, and employment compensation. Likewise, specific examples that lower the relevance of secondary data for marketing research were noted in the prior chapter regarding media versus government data, and demographic information about income, education, and ethnicity.

ACCURACY OF SECONDARY DATA

Accuracy of secondary data is more serious than recency and relevance. Data that are not recent or relevant are readily apparent by their age, categories, and units and can be omitted or restricted quickly. However, inaccurate data usually are more difficult to identify, although people using secondary data are not defenseless.[1] First, they can assume accuracy and use the data, assume some inaccuracy and use the data with qualifications, or assume unacceptable inaccuracy and avoid the data. Second, there are specific actions that can be taken in regard to accuracy of secondary data.

Inaccurate secondary data can be accidental or intentional. Accidental inaccuracies can arise at any stage and activity of the marketing research process. They can be subtle, serious, or as simple as an obvious transposition when reporting numbers, such as $1,924.00 instead of $9,194.00. However, all these inaccuracies pose problems because the current researchers are not likely to be able to determine how precisely each of the initial research stages and activities were conducted.

Intentional inaccuracies also occur in secondary data. They range from slanted interpretations that support a particular interest to outright distorting and misreporting of data. For example, governments and government officials may be motivated to enhance data that favorably influence marketing decisions about expanding business operations in their area of jurisdiction. In fact, some of the secondary data provided to Guinness Brewing Company executives were suspiciously favorable in encouraging the expansion under consideration.

Table 3.1 lists actions and considerations to help in determining the accuracy of secondary data. These include asking standard questions (who, what, why, where, when, and how), conducting cross-check verifications, and considering source credibility in an attempt to arrive at the correct decisions and assumptions.[2]

Standard Questions

Whether or not researchers doubt the accuracy of particular secondary data, they should ask themselves the standard list of questions—who, what, why, where, when, and how—before relying on the data.

Who conducted the initial research? Is this source credible in regard to its reputation for expertise and trustworthiness? If a sample was used to collect information from, who comprised the sample?

What is stated? Is the content reasonable and logical? Are the findings consistent? Were the proper type of data collected, such as quantitative versus nonquantitative? Were the results reported in an understandable, well-organized manner?

Why was the initial research conducted and why was it reported? Are the findings or data self-serving, as for example, those of the cigarette trade association, the Tobacco Institute, that reported no relationship between smoking and health.

Where was the initial research conducted? What sources did it use? Are those sources credible? For data specific to other countries, is it plausible that the initial researcher had the resources and mobility to have collected the data on-site?

Table 3.1
Evaluating Secondary Data

POTENTIAL COMPLICATIONS

Age of Data
Categories of Data
   Income
   Education
   Ethnicity
Units of Data
Accuracy of Data

ACTIONS TO TAKE

Standard questions regarding the data

   Who
   What
   Why
   Where
   When
   How

Cross-check verifications of the data

When was the initial research conducted? Are the dates when the data collection began and ended clearly presented?

How was the initial research conducted? Is the methodology clearly described? Was the sample properly composed, sized, and selected? Were the best data collection and the best data analysis techniques used?

The source of data and distance from the source should receive special attention. The farther data are from the source, the more difficult it is to judge quality and the more likely that inaccuracies are present. With each source succession, accounts of the original procedure usually become less detailed and different. In addition, errors occur in increasing numbers, as a function of interpreting and recording, with each successive reporting.

Accuracy is greatly enhanced when data are obtained from the *original source* as opposed to subsequent sources. The original source is the earliest source available for specific secondary data. In most cases it is the individual or organization whose name is associated with originating the data. A *subsequent source* is a source dated later then the original source of specific secondary data. In most cases, the subsequent source is the individual or organization who is reporting the information from an original source. For example, the original source for magazine and journal articles is the author and publication in which the information was first published, and not authors who paraphrase the original source in a subsequent article.

Cross-Check Verification

When possible, the accuracy of secondary data should be verified through a *cross-check verification*—a technique for verifying the accuracy of secondary data by examining consistency between two independent sources. Data from one source (individual or organization) is compared with corresponding data from another source. The two sources should always be independent of each other. There are two possible actions when a cross-check reveals an inconsistency. If an inconsistency occurs, attempts should be made, first, to determine either the reasons or, second, to determine which data are most likely to be correct. If neither question can be answered, a cost-benefit decision must be made about the risk of using potentially inaccurate data.

Source Credibility

Secondary data are no different than any other data or information that is communicated. The accuracy (actual and perceived) depends on numerous factors embodied by the source and, more precisely, by source credibility. If a source of secondary data is not credible, the accuracy of the data should be questioned by those who conduct the marketing research project and those who use the subsequent information to assist their decision making.

Factors that determine credibility are trustworthiness and expertise. Trustworthiness is, in turn, impacted by objectivity. (Another, closely related, aspect of source credibility is source succession.)

Source Trustworthiness

If secondary data appear self-serving to the source or in any other way not objective, the accuracy is open to skepticism. An example is a business that reports or publishes data that in effect endorses its own products or faults a competitor's products. Consider the recent controversy over the marketing of cigarettes. The medical profession has published studies with overwhelming evidence that document the health dangers of smoking, including those of second-hand smoke. However, at the same time, the largest tobacco companies, as well as the Tobacco Institute (an industry trade association), have published studies showing no causal relationship between smoking and negative health effects. Surely, data presented in the latter studies should be viewed with skepticism given their apparent self-serving nature.

Source Expertise

Accuracy is more open to skepticism when the expertise of the source is open to question. Expertise is also impacted by the research design used to collect, analyze, and report the data. Therefore, it is important to have a detailed account of the research process employed.

If the research process is unknown, then the people associated with the current marketing research project must speculate by using whatever informational clues are available. This speculation should include a reasonable determination whether the person, or organization conducting the original research was knowledgeable about the marketing research process, including its strengths, weaknesses, and limitations. To help achieve this determination, a lengthy list of questions can be posed concerning the activities associated with each of the major components of the marketing research process: data type, sample type, data collection, and data analysis.

Additional questions can be posed concerning activities associated with respective subcomponents. For example: Was the proper type of data collected originally? Should qualitative or quantitative data have been collected? Was the sample properly composed, sized, and selected? Was the best data collection technique used, and were related procedures properly conducted? Once collected, were the data analyzed with the most suitable techniques, and were the techniques conducted properly? Are the results reported in an understandable well-organized manner? Are the data consistent?

Source Succession

The farther from the source of the data, the more difficult it is to judge the quality of that data and the more likely the data are to be inaccurate. Therefore, to increase the accuracy of secondary data, the data should be obtained from the original source as opposed to a subsequent source.

NOTES

1. For additional ideas about the accuracy of secondary data, see Herbert Jacob, *Using Published Data: Errors and Remedies* (Beverly Hills, CA: Sage Publications, 1984); Robert W. Joselyn, *Designing the Marketing Research Project* (New York: Petrocelli/Charter, 1977); and Robert Ferber and P. J. Verdoorn, *Research Methods in Economics and Business* (New York: Macmillan, 1962).

2. See note 1.

4

Internal Secondary Data

A huge amount of secondary data exists, with more being developed continually. The sources of that data can be reasonably categorized as either internal or external. This chapter focuses on internal secondary data, while external secondary data are the focus of the next chapter (Chapter 5).

INTERNAL AND EXTERNAL

Internal secondary data are secondary data whose (original) source was within the organization for which the current marketing research project is conducted. These data are part of an organization's formal marketing information system, which includes standard information available from marketing, accounting, and finance operations. Another dimension of these data involves reports from prior marketing research projects. Their value was expressed well by the director of marketing research at Kraft Foods:

> Key learnings [of past marketing research projects] can help you develop a competitive advantage for your company. By examining your combined learnings you may discover things that other companies have yet to learn. Or you can learn to be

more productive or cost effective and lower your research costs. Or you may learn something that helps you skip steps or speeds your development process.[1]

These data provide robust information when organized as an *internal data base*—a computer data base that is located within the organization for which the current marketing research project is being conducted.[2] Their use can help:

- Evaluate opportunities for marketing new products and services.

- Identify a company's best selling or most profitable products and services.

- Formulate marketing strategy by identifying most and least profitable customers, as well as potential customers.

- Analyze price sensitivity among different target markets.

Consider American Express, where researchers can access the company's large internal data base to obtain information about current and past customers.[3] The data base can reveal quickly activities of its credit card holders via customer credit card purchases. For instance, it can identify people who, in a certain time period, traveled to certain parts of the world, purchased goods at certain types of stores, and attended certain types of entertainment.

Source is a key word in the definition of internal secondary data. Even though secondary data might exist within the organization for which a current project is conducted, if the source is outside the organization, the data are not internal secondary data. For example, an organization might maintain various files of photocopied scholarly journal articles. When particular secondary data are needed for a current marketing research project, the respective researcher can go to these internal files. However, these internal files do not represent internal secondary data.

Internal secondary data is by and large proprietary information. The typical business protocol is to control the confidentiality of this information. Part of this control involves determining levels of confidentiality and availability. For example, some internal data are restricted to a few key executives, other data are restricted to certain departments in the organization, and still others are available to the public. The public information represents carefully selected internal data.

Regardless of the level of confidentiality, all data may be of value to a current marketing research project. Examples of internal secondary data regularly available to the public, and yet still valuable for marketing research, include corporate annual reports; impersonal communications to stockholders; publications aimed at employees, customers, or government institutions; and various information disseminated via announcements through public relations personnel.

The types of internal secondary data of value to current marketing research projects are many. Rather than list precise names for each, it is more beneficial to consider the two major kinds of internal secondary data that embody these data: (1) existing internal secondary data and (2) created internal secondary data.

EXISTING INTERNAL SECONDARY DATA

Existing internal secondary data are data that exist in the course of routine business operations in an organization. These data involve documents that are routinely prepared by standard operating procedures of accounting, finance, and marketing personnel. When a marketing information system (MIS) is constructed, these existing internal secondary data are the building blocks.

Marketing

Marketing operations, as might be expected, provide the most secondary data of direct value to a current marketing research project. Helpful documents prepared routinely in the context of marketing operations include:

Cash register receipts,

Call reports of salespersons,

Customer complaint records,

Customer records (any and all),

Sale invoices,

Service records, and

Warranty cards.

Reports of prior marketing research projects are another helpful type of document. These reports are similar to the already mentioned documents because they are internal secondary data. However, they are different because they are documents that are not routinely prepared.

Analogous to all secondary data, past marketing research projects do pertain exactly to the current project. However, these reports are likely to provide at least some pertinent information which can improve the efficiency and effectiveness of the current project.

Finance

Financial personnel maintain a host of records which, depending on needs of the current marketing research project, can provide valuable information. For example, financial records routinely include classifications of sales revenue, direct sales expenses, overhead sales costs, and profits categorized by products, geographic markets, customers, type of trade, unit of sales organization, and so forth. Additional files contain information about credit transactions. Other relevant data for a current marketing research project include information about product returns and allowances, credit reports, and credit applications.

There are no special statements used exclusively by finance departments. However, helpful finance-type reports include capital budgets (reports involving the allocation of capital to various investments), cash budgets, statements of cash flow, and reports involving alternative sources of financing and their costs. Furthermore, one or more of the many ratios routinely calculated and used by finance personnel can serve as relevant existing internal secondary data. Such ratios pertain to profitability, liquidity, and leverage according to market prices or accounting numbers.

Accounting

Routine responsibilities of accounting personnel include maintaining sales invoices for the purpose of external financial reporting. This information can provide valuable secondary data for a current marketing research project. For example, the data often identify measures of past performance according to customer types, geographical locations, distribution channels, and company products. This identification for marketing research purposes is particularly easy if an organization's accounting system utilizes a modular data base that is suitably coded.

Accounting personnel routinely prepare material that, depending on the situation, may be relevant secondary data for current marketing research projects. For example, each of the four basic financial statements prepared by accounting personnel should be considered: (1) profit/loss statement (the income or operating statement), (2) balance sheet, (3) statement of cash flow, and (4) statement of retained earnings (statement of owners' equity in a proprietorship or partnership).

CREATED INTERNAL SECONDARY DATA

There is a fine line between the preparation of data, as discussed previously, and the transformation of data. At the point when preparation becomes more a case of processing and transforming than preparation, the existing internal secondary data are more appropriately referred to as *created internal secondary data*. Created internal secondary data are existing internal secondary data that have been processed into a format that is useable as marketing research information. It is a value-adding process in that routine documents from such departments as accounting, finance, and marketing are transformed into information of value to current marketing research projects.

The payoff resulting from these preparation efforts can be a valuable sales or cost analysis according to customer type and product purchase. Consider the situation of one of the leading companies in the mail order business: Dell Computers, with headquarters in Austin, Texas. Several months prior to the time of this example, the company had experienced a decline in sales. One response might be to commission a marketing research project with the objective of investigating marketing strategy decisions that focus on advertising effectiveness. By analyzing existing information (internal secondary data), the company might discover that a certain percent, such as 80 percent, of their annual mail order sales came in response to "double truck" (two-page) advertisements placed in issues of *InfoWorld* computer magazine during the fall and winter months. With this information they could adjust their marketing strategy accordingly.

Value-Adding Process

Some preparation is always necessary for using existing internal secondary data. Even data obtained from standard operating procedures of marketing personnel have to be prepared. The preparation depends on the situation but usually involves various types of data aggregating, disaggregating, or tabulating. A later phase in this value-adding process is to utilize the created internal secondary data in making an internal data base.

An *internal data base* is located within the organization for which a current marketing research project is being conducted. The difference between created internal secondary data and an internal data base is a fine line. It is largely a function of organizing the former into a logical body of information and entering that information into a computer as specified.

An internal data base can be a rich source of information for a current marketing research project. For example, it can provide information to:

- Evaluate opportunities for marketing new products and services.

- Identify a company's best selling or most profitable products and services.

- Analyze the price sensitivity among different target markets.

- Formulate marketing strategy by identifying the most and least profitable customers, and potential customers.[4]

Consider, for example, American Express. A person conducting a marketing research project for that company can access its large internal data base to obtain specific information about current and past customers. In part, because of the type of business, accessing the American Express data base for a marketing research project can quickly reveal the activities of credit card holders via the customers' credit card purchases.[5]

Marketing Information System Comparison

Using an internal data base by way of created internal secondary data is closely aligned with the concept of marketing information systems. Both involve transforming rather basic, routine, internal information into marketing research information that to assist marketing decision makers. However, there are at least two major differences.

First, in the context of a marketing information system (MIS), these data are provided continuously, while in the context of a marketing research project, the data are collected, processed, and provided on an intermittent or one-time basis for the current marketing research project.

Second, these data in an MIS context are an end in themselves and are directly available to assist the marketing decision maker, whereas in the current project context, these data are a means to an end. They are part of a marketing research project. While they might ultimately assist a user of the current marketing research project, they are first collected, analyzed, and reported by the marketing researcher involved with the project. Furthermore, as a means to an end, there is another reason why these data are not provided directly to the decision maker: they are used first to form the foundation and context in which primary data are later collected, analyzed, and reported. It is then, in combination with primary data, that these created internal secondary data are presented.

EXISTING INTERNAL DATA BASES

There are two types of internal data bases: created and existing. A *created internal data base* is created specially for the current marketing research project, while an *existing internal data base* exists as part of an MIS or as part of the organization's overall marketing operations. In this latter position, an existing data base might exist as part of the direct marketing efforts of an organization.

Accessing existing internal data bases can provide an immense amount of information for a current marketing research project. In fact, an existing data base can provide a much greater volume of information than an internal data base created specifically for the current marketing research project. The reason for this greater volume is that existing internal data bases are likely to be a culmination of efforts and data amassed over a much longer term than that associated with any one marketing research project.

Consider, for example, some of the largest internal data bases.[6] At the low end of the largest data bases is Kimberly Clark. As the marketer of "Huggies" diapers, this organization maintains names and related information for about 10 million new mothers. Kraft General Food Inc. lists information for about 25 million people in a data base, Citicorp lists about 30 million people, and the Ford Motor organization has about 50 million people indexed.

Subsequent Use

An existing internal data base is useful for a current marketing research project. In turn, a data base created specially for a current marketing research project can also be useful for creating or enhancing an existing data base. This created data base then has two uses in regard to an existing data base: (1) as a component of a marketing information system in the context of marketing research and (2) as the foundation for overall marketing strategy.

Component

As a component of a marketing research MIS, the current data base can serve a continuing function in the form of the data base component of an MIS. In fact, after completion of the current marketing research project, the created internal data base should then become part of the organization's existing internal data base. Then, this created data base can be accessed later if in the future, another current marketing research project is conducted.

If the organization does not yet have an existing internal data base, then the data base created for the current marketing research project can be a useful component in establishing an ongoing internal data base. The logic for this use begins with the fact that the effort to establish an internal data base for a current marketing research project is substantial and represents a less-than-optimal allocation of resources to fail to fully maximize that effort by having it serve a second function. Therefore, depending on amount of effort, scope of the data base, and other organization interests, subsequent uses for a specially created data base for a current marketing research project should always be explored. In the best-case scenario, a subsequent use will be found so that the effort already expended will become a long term investment rather than a one time expense.

Foundation

As the foundation for marketing strategy, the data base created for a current marketing research project can serve as a key influence in *data base marketing*, a marketing strategy in which organizations utilize names, addresses, and other customer information in their efforts to facilitate exchange with their customers. Since such information might have been assembled in a created data base, the organization might seriously consider now using that data base information to incorporate data base marketing or direct marketing into their overall marketing strategy. As a point of information, *direct marketing* is a term used synonymously with data base marketing and, in practice, the two terms are used interchangeably.

Developing an Internal Data Base

There are many ways to develop an internal data base comprised of secondary data for use in a current marketing research project. One way is to process the created internal secondary data into an organized body of computer information. By organizing the created internal secondary data into computer format, an internal data base is made. Another way is to make a subsequent use of the data base created for a current marketing research project. Both of these ways are intermittent, since they are part of a marketing research project which, by definition, is intermittent. However, there is also a continuous way.

Continuous efforts of development are almost always done for the purpose of developing an ongoing data base rather than a data base designed only for the current marketing research project. One approach here is to operate customer clubs. For example, several years ago I became involved in a marketing research project for the Disney Corporation. The objective was to explore the potential for a "Disney Club" to provide Disney fans with various "goodies" in return for an annual membership fee. Through this club, the Disney Corporation would develop a corresponding data base of customer names, addresses, and related information.

Using the context (or pretense) of a membership club is now a common approach for collecting names and related information to develop a data base. For example, to establish a data base within the Adolph Coors Company, frequent buyers of Coors beer are invited to join "Club Coors."[7] Throughout the Burger King empire, 50,000 kids a day provide their names, addresses, and related information to become members of the "Kids Club." For the data base at Kraft foods, new members of "Cheese & Macaroni Club" are given a collection of items that include an embossed hat, bracelet, shoelaces, and stickers. To become a member requires a small cost, three proofs of purchase, and a completed membership form. While such data bases may seem irrelevant to those outside the organization, it apparently is a success (as Table 4.1 indicates).[8]

The development of data bases is an ongoing process that is enhanced through the continuation of various membership club programs. Other enhancements occur through refining and adding additional information to the names already in a data base. For example, Quaker foods in late 1990 mailed out over 5 million coupons.[9] When the coupons were redeemed, electronic scanners at the stores noted a coded number that identifies individual households. Accompanying purchase information was then provided to marketing personnel at the Quaker company. From this information, follow-up mailings can be targeted to which households made specific purchases ranging from pet food to children's products to everything in between.

Table 4.1
"Macaroni and Cheese" Data Base Is a Success

Having children join a "macaroni and cheese club" in order to establish a respective data base may initially seem silly—but evidence verifies the idea. To begin, the Kraft Foods Company encourages children to register their name and address by joining the company's "macaroni and cheese club." As members of the club, the children receive a variety of nominal gifts. In turn, the company can follow-up with promotional mailings. Their motivation is based on the fact that family purchase behavior really is influenced heavily by the children in a family, and if children can be influenced to prefer Kraft Macaroni and Cheese, the children's family is likely to purchase the product.

A study by Simmons Market Bureau Research was quite revealing in this regard. First, the study showed that three out of five parents with children between the ages of 6 and 11 take their children with them when they go grocery shopping. Second, among the influences that children have, the Simmons study reported that in 25 percent of these households, children controlled the selection of macaroni and cheese products, as well as snacks including ice cream, corn and tortilla chips, soft drinks, and frozen pizza.

It should be noted that Simmons Market Bureau Research found even greater influence by children in other product categories. For example, in almost 50 percent of households with children between ages 6 and 11, parents consider the children as experts on such products as breakfast cereal, cookies, candy, and chewing gum.

NOTES

1. Larry P. Stanek, "Keeping Focused on the Consumer while Managing Tons of Information," in *Presentations from the 9th Annual Marketing Research Conference* (Chicago: American Marketing Association, 1988), pp. 62-70.

2. See "Desktop Marketing at Your Fingertips," *Business Marketing*, August 1988, p. 58. A data base is merely "a body of information stored in a computer, which can process it and from which particular pieces of information can be retrieved when required." Both data bases and marketing information systems can involve transforming rather basic, routine, internal information into marketing research information to assist marketing decision makers. Therefore, since an internal data base is closely aligned the marketing information systems, it may be helpful to refer back to the earlier chapter discussing marketing information systems.

3. "Database Marketing Alters Landscape," *Marketing News*, November 7, 1988, p. 1.

4. "Desktop Marketing at Your Fingertips," p. 58.

5. "Database Marketing Alters Landscape," p. 1.

6. "Database Marketing Alters Landscape," p. .

7. "Databases Uncover Brands' Biggest Fans," *Advertising Age*, February 19, 1990, pp. 3, 73.

8. "Children Have Pull on Shopping Carts," *The Wall Street Journal*, 73, no. 163 (June 3, 1992); p. B-1.

9. "Databases Uncover Brands' Biggest Fans," pp. 3, 73.

5

External Secondary Data

As noted in Chapter 4, the sources of the huge amount of existing and continually developing pool of secondary data can be categorized as internal or external. The focus of this current chapter is on external secondary data which, in addition, can be either public or private.

External secondary data are secondary data whose source is outside the organization for which the current marketing research project is being conducted. Individual options number in the millions since they include books, journals, magazines, data bases, government agencies, media organizations, newspapers, trade associations, television networks, news bureaus, and business enterprises actively developing more information reports.

PUBLIC AND PRIVATE

External secondary data can be generally classified as public or private. *Public external secondary data* are external secondary data available at nominal cost or free. The data are plentiful and locating desired data can require substantial time and effort. The data are normally received from an office directly associated with the source or from public libraries. The source is generally the government: federal, state, city, or local.

These data also can be received from business enterprises for additional charge. The business enterprises repackage information from the original form. This service saves researchers time and effort by isolating desired information and providing it in desired format (e.g., specified tables and columns, printed hard copy, computer disks compatible with word processing software, etc.). An example are companies that reorganize the massive census bureau data to meet more specialized needs. Three companies are *Donnelley Demographics* (available through such vendors as DIALOG), *The Sourcebook of Zip Code Demographics* (distributed by the Gale Research Company),[1] and *SuperSite* (available through such vendors as CompuServe and Chase Econometrics).

Private external secondary data are external secondary data available for a market value fee. These data are obtained from private business enterprises that are not affiliated with government agencies or government funding. Their cost is less than respective primary data because their distribution is through a *standardized marketing information service*—a business enterprise that provides the same secondary data to all interested parties. An example is the Nielsen Television Audience Viewing Index.

With techniques such as electrical-mechanical devices attached to televisions, the Nielsen company determines the number of people who watch particular television programs and then reports the data as a *television rating percentage*—the percent of those households that own televisions that had them tuned to a particular television program, and as a *television share percentage*—the percent of all televisions switched on that were tuned to a particular television program. Once collected, this information is tabulated and sold to all four of the major American television networks (ABC, CBS, Fox, and NBC), as well as to other interested parties such as advertising agencies and other businesses in the marketing and media industries.

Private, external secondary data provided by standardized marketing information services embodies a diverse industry. Tools, techniques, and business enterprises range from the long-established to recent developments made possible by the latest technological developments. For example, geodemography (which provides census data according to geographical areas) is feasible in its latest forms because of improved computer technology. Table 5.1 lists a sampling of current tools and techniques, while Table 5.2 identifies some of the major business enterprises and indicates their products.

GENERAL GROUPS

The profusion of sources for external secondary data applicable to marketing research can be reasonably categorized into six general groups: (1) books, (2) periodicals, (3) government, (4) media, (5) trade associations and (6) business enterprises.

Books

Books can provide an impressive amount of information. However, the content is outdated quickly in areas where changes occur rapidly. Since library catalogs list only holdings of that particular library, a noteworthy publication is *Books in Print*. Books not in a library's holdings can be usually obtained through the interlibrary loan service or purchased through a local book store. In some instances a book's author might be contacted directly for additional information about a topic.

Periodicals

Periodicals can provide scholarly or mass media information, and can be categorized as journals or magazines, respectively. Journals publish articles that usually have passed the scrutiny of a peer review process and they tend to appeal to a small audience that is knowledgeable about the topic. Articles published in magazines are not subjected to a similar peer review and tend to appeal to a wider audience.

Information of value to marketing research can be found in journals and magazines in fields adjacent to marketing (such as psychology, sociology, finance, accounting, management, etc.), as well as periodicals specific to marketing. Articles published in periodicals not readily available can be usually obtained through an interlibrary loan service. Moreover, in some instances, the author of an article may be contacted directly for additional information.

Table 5.1
Sampling of Current Tools and Techniques for Providing
Private, External Secondary Data

Audimeter—Electronic device attached to a television set, which records the time and channel of operation and then transmits this information to a central computer.

Geodemography—Marketing information is provided based on census data and other data by geographic areas. Typically, the presentation is in the form of a computer-designed map.

Standard Industrial Classification codes (SIC codes)—This elaborate system was developed by the American government in collaboration with the U.S. Census. It is a widely used and comprehensive system that reports business information, including number of employees and total sales for businesses throughout the United States.

Store audits—A system in which field workers (i.e., auditors) take inventory of products in a sample of retail stores. As well as counting stocked products, examinations are made of transaction receipts between manufacturers, wholesales, and retailers.

Diary panels—A system in which information is collected from the same group of people over a period of time.

Scanners—An electronic mechanism that reads, records, and processes the Universal Product Code (UPC) for products, prints the name and price of products on a sales receipt for consumers, and records the sale and change in inventory for management.

People meters—A later generation of audimeter. It attempts to measure who is watching television, as well as the time of operation and channel to which a television is tuned.

Single-source data—A system that provides data about the relationship between television viewing and product purchases.

Table 5.2
Sampling of Business Enterprises and Their Products

Automated Customer Evaluation Service (ACES)—ACES is a product of Donnelley Marketing. In cooperation with Citicorp Credit Services, it provides customer profile information based on sales receipts for purchases made using MasterCard and Visa credit cards.

BehaviorScan—A single-source data system operated by Information Resources. Once a household agrees to participate, it is issued an identification card that is scanned when purchases are made. BehaviorScan provides information about a household's purchases by brand, size and price, according to the demographic characteristics and exposure to marketing efforts such as coupons, newspaper advertisements, and point-of-purchase displays, etc.

Consumer Mail Panel (CMP)—Operated by Market Facts Inc., CMP is a panel of 275,000 households, from which samples are selected to participate in custom-designed marketing research projects.

Dun's Market Identifiers (DMI)—DMI provides marketing information from Dun and Bradstreet. It lists over 4 million enterprises, which are updated monthly and includes business information arranged by SIC codes.

Dun's Market Identifiers (DMI 2+2 Enhancement System)—This system is a more precise version of Dun's Market Identifiers (DMI) and provides greater target market information.

Mediamark Research—Mediamark focuses on product usage and media exposure: magazines, newspapers, radio, and television. Product usage involves a sample of approximately 20,000 respondents involving over 450 products and over 5,500 brands.

Table 5.2 continued

NFO Research, Inc.—NFO maintains a national panel of consumers, with whom it communicates with by mail/post. The company conducts custom-designed marketing research projects among its panel members.

National Purchase Diary (NPD)—NPD is the largest consumer diary panel in the United States, with more than 15,000 households which report monthly purchases in about fifty product categories.

Nielsen Retail Index—A store audit system by the A. C. Nielsen Company. Information reported includes sales volume, retail prices, store displays, and marketing activities.

Nielsen Television Index—A system that uses audiometers and people meters to measure the number of households that watched a particular channel at particular times.

R. L. Polk and Urban Decision Systems (UDS)—UDS provides consumer information according to geographic areas. UDS is especially valuable when used in combination with the "Vehicle Origin Survey" (also a product of R. L. Polk).

R. L. Polk and Urban Decision Systems Vehicle Origin Survey—Part of the R. L. Polk and Urban Decision Systems (UDS), the Vehicle Origin Survey provides data on license plate numbers for cars in parking areas. With motor vehicle registration files, the owners' geographic areas are identified to provide unobtrusive information about people who patronize a particular shopping area or mall.

Prizm (Potential Ratings for Zip Markets)—A product of the Claritas company, Prizm divides the United States into 250,000 areas (or neighborhoods) and identifies them with one of forty categories of consumer behavior and life-styles.

Table 5.2 continued

SCANTRACK—A scanner system operated by the A. C. Nielsen company. It supplements the Nielsen Retail Index by providing weekly sales data from a nationwide sample of stores equipped with scanning devices.

Starch Readership Service—Starch focuses on advertising effectiveness for promotions in magazines and newspapers. It annually interviews over 100,000 people, in regard to about 75,000 advertisements placed in roughly 1,000 issues of various consumer magazines, business publications, and newspapers.

Simmons Media/Marketing Service—The Simmons product focuses on product usage and media exposure. The four mediums of magazine, television, newspaper, and radio are all covered with a sample of about 19,000 respondents. Information is collected on over 800 product categories.

Government

Secondary data of value to marketing research are provided by all levels of the government: country (federal/national), regional (state and multistate), and local (county, city, and municipality). Actions to locate relevant government information include directly contacting elected officials at all levels of government. Additionally, an enlightening list of information provided by the American government is identified in such books as Matthew Lesko's *Lesko's Info-Power Sourcebook*.[2]

Media

Media organizations (television, radio, newspapers, magazines, billboards, etc.) collect information about audiences and news topics. These sources of secondary data can be either general audience media (e.g., *Time* and *Newsweek* magazines) or specialized marketing and business media (e.g., *Advertising Age, Marketing Week, The Wall Street Journal,* and *Business Week*). Locating media information include contacting the organizations directly.

Trade Associations

Practically all products are identified with a particular industry, and practically every industry has trade associations that collect data about products, consumers, and industry trends. These data will be often provided to those interested at nominal or no fee. Most libraries have comprehensive directories that list trade association names and contact information (addresses, telephone numbers, fax numbers, and computer e-mail addresses). In addition, the company that produces or distributes a product can be contacted directly to identify the respective trade association.

Business Enterprises

Many business enterprises market secondary data. Tables 5.1 and 5.2 present a sampling of these businesses: Consumer Mail Panel, Dun's Market Identifiers, Prizm, Simmons Media/Marketing Service, and similar services. Three additional businesses are:

1. Selling Areas: Marketing, Incorporated (SAMI)— Provides data about product movement from distributor warehouses into retail stores.

2. Nielsen Retail Index Service—Provides data about retail sales volume, inventories, brands, out-of-stock situations, prices, etc.

3. Burgoyne, Inc.—Provides data pertaining to different types of retailers that include convenience stores, grocery stores, drug stores, mass merchandisers, and hardware stores.

Actions to locate such businesses include (1) asking the local chapter, national headquarters, or international headquarters of relevant professional organizations (such as the American Marketing Association or Marketing Research Association), (2) scanning advertisements and periodical directories published in pertinent trade magazines (such as *Marketing News* or *Quirk's Marketing Research Review*), (3) consulting telephone directory yellow pages, and (4) seeking referrals from business associates.

NOTES

1. The Gale Research Company is located at Gale Research, Inc., 835 Penobscot Bldg., Detroit, MI 48226; telephone: 800-877-GALE (800-877-4253).

2. Matthew Lesko, *Lesko's Info-Power Sourcebook* (Kensington, MD: Information U.S.A., 1990).

6

Locating Secondary Data

Standard actions to locate information about, or provided by, any of the groups of secondary data sources (books, periodicals, government, media, trade associations and business enterprises) involve the use of:

Colleagues,

Library catalog,

Librarians,

Reference indexes,

Computer data bases, and

Direct contact.

Focusing on the topic and key words that are most related to the objective of the current marketing research project will yield the most productive search for information, regardless of sources investigated and actions taken. One action that practitioners always should take when searching for information is to ask colleagues. Researchers also should peruse the library catalog (which, at larger libraries, and increasingly at almost all universities, is computerized in a system formally known as OPAC for On-Line Public Access Catalog), speak with librarians, scan reference indexes, which may be in print or on computer (such as *The Wall Street Journal Index* or *Business Periodicals Index*), access computer data bases (on-line or CD-ROM), and contact sources directly as appropriate.

STANDARD INDUSTRIAL CLASSIFICATION SYSTEM

To search for American business-to-business data (also known as industrial or industry data), key numbers assigned by the Standard Industrial Classification System (SIC Codes) are also important since they are widely used both inside and outside government to record and retrieve data.

This system, commonly referred to as the SIC Codes, was devised by the American government as a way to uniformly classify organizations based on their economic activity. Details are published in the *Standard Industrial Classification Manual*, which is available at many libraries and from the United States Office of Management and Budget in Washington, DC. Examples of sources that provide data according to SIC Codes are the *U.S. Census of Manufacturers*, *U.S. Industrial Outlook and County Business Patterns*, *Predicasts*, and *Dun and Bradstreet's Market Identifiers*.

LIBRARIES AND LIBRARIANS

The quantities of secondary data, and even their sources, multiply at geometric rates, with commensurate changes in the procedures and technology used to archive and retrieve these data. Therefore, specialists in the form of librarians are required in this extremely dynamic field. A marketing researcher cannot possibly have the expertise about secondary data that is possessed by competent librarians who are respective specialists. For example, a library index, which is a data base used to locate specific existing information, is an essential tool for marketing researchers. However, through the late 1970s, these indexes were only available in printed form. Searching through such publications was both an inefficient and ineffective way to locate useful information. Now, almost all indexes are computerized data bases that are accessed through CD-ROM, laser disk, or on-line via satellite transmission, with more developments in progress.

The numbers of these computer data bases have exploded concurrently, such that a competent librarian can provide nearly priceless direction. Regardless if the marketing researcher is working in a local city library, university library, or in-house corporate library, librarians can help access data from literally around the world. If the desired information is not held at a particular library, they likely can obtain it through either interlibrary loan or via a computer data base.

Although external secondary data and their sources are located literally around the world, they are readily accessible at sites convenient to almost all marketing researchers, regardless of their own location. The key consideration to this access are the library and, of course, the librarians. Libraries and the librarians who work within them are the best friends for marketing researchers involved with projects for which secondary data are utilized.

There are three types of libraries that are especially valuable to marketing researchers. These are the (1) local city library, (2) university library, and (3) in-house corporate library. Depending on the situation, one or the other may be more convenient, but the function of each is to provide information via secondary data. Any one library can only house a fraction of available external secondary data. If the desired information is not stored at a particular library, which may be the one of closest proximity or greatest convenience to the individual conducting the marketing research project, that library is likely to be able to obtain it. It can accomplish this task either through interlibrary loan or by working with a computer data base.

DATA BASES

Among the means to locate information, data bases comprised of computer indexes and directories are the most effective and efficient means for obtaining secondary data. In fact, data bases are the heart of the process of locating external secondary data. A *data base* is defined as a body of information stored in a computer, which can process it and from which particular pieces of information can be retrieved when required. In the context of external secondary data, that definition is no different.

Technically, a data base need not be on a computer, but practically speaking, data bases almost always are. For marketing researchers, computerized data bases are essential to locate the most useful information in the most efficient and effective manner. In this procedure, they serve as indexes or directories indicating where specific secondary information is located. While data bases vary in recency and scope, they generally provide reference citations and summaries of articles and reports from around the world.

Computerized Technology

A data base (as defined in this book and in most other disciplines) implies computer accessibility. In other words, all data bases are not technically computerized, but for all practical purposes, the mention of a data base almost always assumes that it is computerized. With this understanding, data bases can be differentiated as either on-line or off-line.

An *on-line database* is computerized and accessed by computer keyboard. The distance between the actual data base and the keyboard operator may be near or far. For example, an on-line data-base of interest to marketing researchers might be located literally next door, on the other side of the world, or anywhere in between. An *off-line database* is a computerized data base that first must be physically loaded by a computer keyboard operator. Thus, the procedure for loading the data base (connecting it to the computer being used) is more important than amount of distance in differentiating between on-line and off-line data bases. It is worthwhile to note here that *portable data base* is a term used synonymously with off-line database and, practically speaking, the two terms are used interchangeably.

Physical Procedures

Computerized data bases are always housed in a storage mechanism accessible by suitable communication facilities. These facilities include proper computer software, hardware, and transmission technology (such as a modem), which allows communication between the user's computer and the central computer through which the data base is accessed. The storage mechanism might be a hard drive disk within a computer, a floppy diskette, CD-ROM, magnetic tape, laser disk, or some other device. When such a data base is accessed on-line, a person or machine (other then the keyboard operator) arranges the appropriate physical configuration at the storage facilities location, which includes loading the storage mechanism into the computer mechanism to permit communication.

When a computer message for information comes into the storage area, a person or machine loads the appropriate storage mechanism (hard drive disk, floppy diskette, laser disk, CD-ROM, etc.) into the appropriate computer mechanism. Obviously, another person or machine is necessary when the data base is in a distant location. Obviously, as well, suitable communication facilities are necessary.

The storage technology for all computerized data bases is the same (e.g., diskettes, CD-ROM, etc.), but not all computerized data bases are distant to the keyboard operator. While a data base and its loading into appropriate computer mechanism might be done next door or thousands of miles away, it might also be done by the individual computer operator him- or herself. For example, many libraries and offices purchase and house their own copy of a data base. In these situations, the marketing researcher is loaned a physical copy (on a diskette, CD-ROM, or other such storage mechanism), which must first be loaded into a computer before beginning a search of the data base for the desired external secondary data.

Common Elements

CD-ROMs, laser disks, digital tape systems, and new, yet to be released, technologies abound, with CD-ROM the most common. One CD-ROM (compact disk read-only memory) stores about the same as 1,500 floppy diskettes, or about 275,000 printed pages. Advantages of the off-line CD-ROM are that a person can load it into a personal computer instead of going on-line, it can be used anywhere and anytime, and there are no additional costs for telephone line charges, connect fees, or searching time. A disadvantage is that CD-ROM data bases are not updated as readily as on-line data bases. Unlike updating an on-line data base, where new information needs only be placed on a central computer, a new CD-ROM must be sent to each owner. Off-line CD-ROMs that are sold to libraries, and other interested parties, must be updated similarly by sending a new copy to each library.

One example of a CD-ROM data base is that sold by the R. H. Donnelley company. That company currently sells CD-ROMs with demographic data, retail sales data, and other data for literally hundreds of product categories according to geographical areas in the United States. The geographical area breakdowns follows the American postal zip code system. A second example of a CD-ROM data base is the TIGER System marketed by the U.S. Census Bureau. TIGER is an acronym for Topologically Integrated Geographic Encoding and Reference System. First available for the 1990 United States census, this data base provides census information for the entire United States population and geographical area.

Distribution Channel

Data bases are marketed like almost any other product. Regardless if they are on-line or off-line, data bases of interest to marketing researchers involve a distribution channel analogous to that of products, in which there are three key characters, the manufacturer, intermediary (wholesaler and retailer), and consumer. In this situation, these are the data base producer, data base vendor, and data base user, respectively.

Data Base Producer

The data base *producer* is the individual who collects, organizes, and transfers data base information into a computer readable format. The producers might be a company, organization, or other entity. Producers either collect, organize, and transfer the information themselves or may instead own the company that performs this work. In other words, data base producers are manufacturers who purchase raw materials, assemble products, and then market the products. This is true for both on-line data base products and off-line products.

A data base producer of a typical (albeit large) product may have a data base with over 1 million citations. In turn, each of these citations might provide bibliography reference information and one or two paragraph summaries (i.e., article abstracts) of the cited material. One example of a data base of value to many marketing researchers is ABA/Inform. The reason for its value is that ABA/Inform provides abstracts of articles that are published in more than 800 business periodicals.

Another example of a valuable data base is Standard and Poor's Corporate Descriptions which provides information on more than 8,000 American corporations that have stock that is publicly held. For these corporations, information includes size in terms of number of employees; names of the officers, directors, and principal stockholders; identification of capital expenditures; and two years of balance sheet information.

Data Base Vendor

The data base *vendor* is the intermediary between the data base producer and the data base user. Data base vendors are wholesalers and retailers, who together "break bulk" and set prices for the consumer. These vendors also modify data bases from producers by packaging and repackaging them as deemed appropriate. For example, some are combined with other data bases, while others are divided into one or more smaller, sometimes more specialized data bases. The result is that a particular data base purchased from different vendors may have differing information and prices. This is true for both on-line products and off-line data products.

One example of a major data base vendor is DIALOG. The company markets over 350 data bases that include both the data bases mentioned earlier (ABA/Inform data base and Standard and Poor's Corporate Descriptions). To present a better picture of the relationship between data bases and data base vendors, Table 6.1 presents a small sampling of products offered by four popular data base vendors: CompuServe, DIALOG (Dialog Information Services), Dow Jones News Services, and the Source.

Data Base User

The data base *user* is the individual that utilizes data base information, in either on-line or off-line form. The user might be a company, organization, or other entity. The researcher may access the data base him- or herself, or the organization in which the researcher is employed may handle this task. Most people's first experience as a data base user is in regard to locating information through a library for a term paper in school. The exposure for marketing researchers is similar, except that the price is different for using such products.

Table 6.1
Sample Data Bases Marketed by Four Major Data Base Vendors

CompuServe

AP [Associated Press] News
Business Information Wire
Compu*U*Store
Microquote (stock information)
Standard & Poor's General Information File
Washington Post
World Book Encyclopedia

DIALOG (Dialog Information Services)

AP News
Books in Print
Disclosure II (business data base)
Electronic Yellow Pages
Magazine Index
Management Contents
Standard & Poor's Corporate Description

Dow Jones News Services

Academic American Encyclopedia
AP News
Cinema Movie Reviews
Comp*U*Store
Current Quotes
Disclosure II
Dow Jones News
Wall Street Journal

Table 6.1 continued

The Source

AP News
Cinema Movie Reviews
Comp*U*Store
Commodity News Service
Employment Service
Management Contents
U.S. News Washington Letter
Travel Services

The price that data base users pay differs according to the vendor or retailer, as well as the quantity of information utilized or purchased. For an on-line data base product, typical direct expenses include the charges for telephone-line usage, a connect charge, and the price for locating and printing the information.

Alternatives

The total number of alternatives available to data base users is huge and growing, but there are directories of data bases to help manage the alternatives. One help is the *Directory of Online Databases*, which is published annually by Gale Research and provides extensive updated listings of computer data bases.[1] Related publications by the same company include the *Directory of Online Databases*, *Directory of Portable Databases*, and *Computer-Readable Databases*. In fact, there are even directories of the directories. For example, the *Directory of Directories*, published by Gale Research, provides information on more than 10,000 business and industrial directories. Three other products marketed by this company that are valuable in marketing research include:

Directory of Special Libraries and Information Centers—Data on 18,000 special libraries and information centers.

Encyclopedia of Associations—Data on more than 20,000 national associations and 3,500 international associations.

International Research Centers Directory—Data on more than 4,000 entities (centers, institutes, etc.) that support research.

Many data base alternatives exist for two reasons. First, there are many individual data bases. As early as 1992, there were more than 5,000 separate on-line data bases accessed through telephone lines and satellite transmissions, as well as over 2,000 separate off-line data bases accessed through CD-ROM, diskette and magnetic tape. Second, the number of alternatives available to users is multiplicative because different vendors bundle their packages of data bases differently.

Attempting to structure many data bases into a meaningful manner for marketing researchers is not an easy task. One approach is consider these data bases as one of several types: numeric, bibliographic, or full text.

Numeric Data Base

A numeric data base contains original data, usually in numerical form and collected through a survey. One example of a numeric data base of value to marketing research is the VALS/MRI combined data base which includes information on nearly 6,000 brands of products. The VALS (values and life-styles) component is a product of Stanford Research Institute and consists of data about attitudes, wants, and beliefs from over 12,000 participants. The MRI component (a product of Medimark Research Incorporated) consists of data about magazine readers, radio listeners, and television viewers from 20,000 adult participants.

Bibliographic Data Base

A bibliographic data base contains an index of published studies and published reports. They sometimes include abstracts or summaries, which might include information about analyses and explanations of the specific studies and reports identified.

One example of a bibliographic data base of value to marketing research projects is FIND/SVP which provides information on more than 11,000 studies conducted by over 500 marketing researchers. Among these studies are marketing research reports about consumer behavior, products, store audits, and worldwide surveys of more than 50 industries.

Full Text Data Base

Within the category of bibliographic data bases, some provide more information then others. A full text data base contains complete articles and reports, in contrast to most types of data bases, which limit their information in one of two ways. One way is to include only bibliography citation information (e.g., article title, periodical name, authors, date, volume number, and page number). A second way is include bibliography citation information combined with a brief summary (i.e., abstract) about each cited item.

One example of a full text data base is the *Harvard Business Review* data base which provides the full text for all articles published in its journal since 1976. Furthermore, it permits searching of its data base by specific product, subject, and industry, as well as by title and company. Other examples are the *New York Times* data base and *Dow-Jones Test-Search Services*.

NOTE

1. Contact information for this company is Gale Research, Inc., 835 Penobscot Building, Detroit, MI 48226; telephone: 800-877-GALE.

PART II

SPECIFIC SOURCES OF SECONDARY DATA

IMPORTANCE OF SPECIFIC SOURCES FOR SECONDARY DATA

A *secondary data source* is any person, publication, or medium, that provides data or information compiled for a purpose other than the current marketing research project. Six common, basic sources of secondary data were identified as books, periodicals, government agencies and offices, media such as television, radio, newspapers, and magazines, trade associations, and business enterprises. These are only basic sources of information.

What the researcher of a particular marketing research project most needs is specific sources that hold the desired information. Since an important aspect of locating desired information is to have an awareness of the specific sources relevant to marketing research and marketing, the focus of the chapters in Part 2 is on specific sources.

In one sense, it is more important to know the basics of secondary data then it is to know specific sources of secondary data (as presented Part 2). The reason is due to the rapid changes occurring throughout the field of secondary data. For example, technologies for locating information and the specific information quickly become outdated and discontinued. In turn, new technologies and new sources of secondary data are created and developed into products of greater value to marketing researchers. Furthermore, data base vendors change their product offerings as business conditions warrant.

However, these changes are more evolutionary than revolutionary. The truism still holds that the more things change, the more they remain the same. Regardless of the changes, it is still necessary to be aware of specific sources of secondary data that exist at this time. Such a dynamic environment is not unique to the secondary data aspect of marketing research. A dynamic environment is the status quo for all of marketing, which should not stop us from the studying it as it stands today. In fact, to be prepared for tomorrow's environments in marketing, marketing research, and secondary data, it is important to be knowledgeable about today's environment even though change is a constant.

INCREASING EASE OF USE

The specific secondary sources listed in this part are quite standard and not likely to be discontinued. What is likely to change is that they will become increasingly easier to locate, access, and utilize. Printed books are continuously being converted to electronic files or data bases, while computer networks to access the data bases are growing accordingly. As a result, a growing number of traditionally printed material is being computerized. Just one example is Project Gutenberg at the University of Illinois, which is currently in the process of converting 10,000 of the most frequently used books into computerized form.[1] Another example is CENDATA, an on-line data base available to access much of the U.S. Census Bureau data, which has traditionally been available only in printed form.

Computer data bases are big business and growing bigger. An indication of their size is the fact that 1992 revenues earned by the electronic data base industry were about $11 billion.[2] Another indication of growth are the projections of 20 percent increases per year, to reach more than $22 billion by 1995.[3] The size and growth mean more than money. Over each of the past ten years, numbers of new computerized data bases have increased by about 25 percent per year and full text data bases have increased by more than 50 percent per year; in addition, since CD-ROMS were first marketed in 1986, they have increased by about 60 percent per year.[4]

INCREASING COMPUTERIZATION

Increasing computerization creates problems and opportunities for marketing researchers. A problem is that the explosion of accessible information can easily prove overwhelming. However, an opportunity is that along with this growth, those who conduct marketing research have access to more secondary data then ever before. Secondary data sources are no longer available only in printed format such as books and microfilm or microfiche at the local library. Increasingly, the secondary data of interest to marketing researchers is available locally in the form of a CD-ROM or at a far distance but easily accessible via computerized on-line data bases.

To make use of distant data bases in the most efficient and effective manner, computerized networks are becoming increasingly important.[5] In fact, in 1992 there were over 1,000 computer networks. Some of the best known include:

INTERNET—a computer network used extensively by libraries. Libraries make information available as their resources permit, and in turn they use information according to their needs. Catalogs, indexes, and full text materials are available.[6]

TELNET—allows a user to interact with the information stored in another computer as if the user directly connected to the remote computer.

ELECTRONIC MAIL ("e-mail") via BITNET—is a storage and forwarding service that allows for transmission of text messages. In its basic form it cannot access other networks. However, it is an extremely efficient means of communication. A message sent from one computer user to another is stored in the recipient's "mailbox" until read. This network connects approximately 2,500 educational institutions and libraries in thirty-two countries.

FTP (FILE TRANSFER PROTOCOL)—is a form of e-mail, albeit a superior form. It is technically a file-sharing protocol that gives users the ability to move files from one part on the INTERNET to another.

A key dimension to making full use of computerized data bases is utilizing respective specialists. This is especially true when a new project or, more typically, a new source of information is desired. As a result, it is becoming increasingly important for marketing researchers to work with personnel who are knowledgeable in internetworking (i.e., working between) systems, procedures, and networks. With the dramatic changes that occur, a marketing researcher cannot be expected to be aware of all new developments.

To go beyond current knowledge, marketing researchers need only to consult a specialist such as competent library personnel. They are specialists in their field and are likely to be the most knowledge about secondary data sources and how to locate them.

CAUTIONARY NOTE

The objective of this part is to present a representative sample of specific secondary data sources. For ease of comprehension, these sources are categorized as follows:

Marketing Specific Information—Chapter 7

Global/Worldwide Information—Chapter 8

American Census Data Information—Chapter 9

Reference Guides—Chapter 9

Industries Information—Chapter 10

Corporate Directory Information—Chapter 10

Investment, Financial, and Economic Information—Chapter 10

Business Information Not Specific to Marketing—Chapter 11

General and Dissimilar Information—Chapter 11

The reader should be alert to at least four considerations in regard to these categorical listings and their sources specifically identified. First, as indicated above, historically printed materials are increasingly being made available in both printed format and a variety of computer formats. Therefore, while many of the descriptions of the sources indicate availability in various computer formats, there are likely more that have occurred between the time this book was printed and the time it is now being read.

Second, any one source may have contents that apply to more than one category. An example is that a data base or any other secondary data source that focuses on a particular country will include data pertaining to other countries.

Third, while a wide variety of specific sources are presented, these are only a sampling of the sources available to, and utilized by, marketing researchers.

Fourth, almost all these specific secondary data sources listed in this part are in the English language, and they are available in printed format unless stated otherwise.

CASE STUDY

Ask "Information on Demand." The president of Information on Demand, Christine Maxwell, contends that if they "can't find the answer, then you never will."[7] The company, with headquarters in Berkeley, California, serves clients around the globe with answers to questions that range from the mundane to the unusual. For example:

What is the per capita income of people living in Texas?

How many people are there in the United States between the ages of twenty-one and thirty-five?

Do the Japanese play basketball? What about chess?

How large a market is there for Christmas trees in Hawaii?

How much beer do people in Vietnam drink? What about Australia? What about South, and even North, Korea?

Is there a market for snake venom? What about bee venom?

To provide these answers, the company is connected to hundreds of computerized data bases. Information on Demand provides clients with the information they desire in times as short as a few hours up to a few weeks. During the longer time periods, clients can call in toll-free for status reports. Once located, the information can be delivered in almost any format the client desires, ranging from a printed copy delivered by mail, special delivery, or fax to information over the telephone.

The services of Information on Demand are not restricted to the hundreds of computerized data bases available to them. There simply are too many other sources of secondary data. Consequently, the company employs staff to travel to libraries and research centers, both local and distant. Furthermore, even when information appears to be found in a data base, it may be only a brief reference to an obscure publication, material at a faraway location, or an entry with a slightly incorrect reference citation. As Maxwell states, "Just finding something in a data base or in a bibliographic list does not mean it is then easy to locate physically." That is only the first step. The next step is often to obtain a copy of the document ranging from, for example, the Film History Library in Los Angeles, the Library of Congress in Washington, DC, or a host of other locations in cities ranging from London, England, to Tokyo, Japan. In fact, Maxwell states that the business "often functions with a detective mentality" to locate and obtain the information requested.

NOTES

1. Michael S. Hart, "Project Gutenberg: Access to Electronic Texts," *Database*, December 1990, p. 7.

2. S. Michael Malinconico, "Information's Brave New World," *Library Journal*, May 1, 1992, pp. 36-40.

3. "Information Services," *1991 Industrial Outlook*, 32nd ed. (Washington, DC: U.S. Department of Commerce, 1991), pp. 27-32.

4. Malinconico, "Information's Brave New World," pp. 36-40.

5. This section is based on personal conversations with numerous library and computer staff personnel at the Hong Kong University of Science and Technology during the author's employment there in 1992. The interested reader should obtain a copy of Brendan P. Kehoe's *Zen and the Art of the Internet: A Beginner's Guide to the Internet* (January 1992, Chester, Pennsylvania, at "brendan@cs.widener.edu"). This is truly an excellent publication for the novice interested in an introduction to computer internetworking in general, and Internet in particular.

6. Two excellent sources of information for the novice internet

user are Bennett Falk, *The Internet Roadmap* (Alameda, CA: SYBEX, 1994); and Daniel P. Dern, *The Internet Guide for New Users* (New York: McGraw-Hill, 1994).

7. Material in this section is based on an article by David Holmstrom, "Christine Maxwell: The Business of Knowledge," *American Way*, March 15, 1987, pp. 19-24.

7

Sources of Information
Specific to Marketing

It might be misleading to designate one part of these secondary data sources as marketing specific because all the specific sources identified in this second part apply to marketing and marketing research. However, the secondary data sources identified in this chapter are particularly germane to topics often helpful to assist in making marketing decisions.

The sources in this chapter pertain almost exclusively to marketing information involving the United States. Respective secondary data of interest to marketing executives and marketing researchers are also available for other countries. Therefore, the interested reader is referred to the secondary data sources identified in Chapter 8, which provide marketing information for countries other than the United States.

UNITED STATES INFORMATION

Adtrack

On-line data base that presents every advertisement of a quarter page or larger from 150 major consumer and business publications.

Its efforts are comprehensive in that they represent over 98 percent of the advertising revenues in major magazine categories. Information provided includes the ability to research a product's share of advertising space, a company's advertising strategy and style, and advertising patterns within certain industries. Advertisements can also be searched according to topics such as product, company, characteristics, content, telephone number, spokesperson, and coupons.

Available through such vendors as DIALOG.

Aging America—Trends and Projections

Provides information about the elderly population in the United States, including their numbers, demographics, employment, health, and income. Included in this information are corresponding thirty-year projections.

Publisher: U.S. Senate Special Committee on Aging and the American Association of Retired Persons (Washington, DC: U.S. Government Printing Office).

American Marketing Association Bibliography Series

Provides annotated bibliographies of special interest to marketing. This information is organized according to topic.

Updates: Periodically.

Publisher: American Marketing Association (Chicago, IL).

Arbitron Information on Demand

On-line data base that provides information on over 200 television markets and over 250 radio markets in the United States. Annual surveys are conducted to collect demographic and psychographic information about television and radio audiences. This data base includes statistics about reach and frequency, in addition to gross impressions and rating points.

Available through such vendors as Control Data and Interactive Market Systems.

Communications Abstracts

Provides information on communications-related reports, books, and articles. Information includes topics such as marketing, public opinion, the media, advertising, small-group communication, and mass media communication.

Updates: Quarterly.

Publisher: Sage Publications (Beverly Hills, CA).

D&B-Dun's Market Identifiers

On-line data base that serves as a directory of public and private businesses in the United States. Companies listed are only those with more than $1 million in annual sales or with five or more employees. All types of companies are indexed, representing almost all types of products. More than two million companies are indexed in this data base, and information is provided on more than thirty searchable facts about each company. For example, information includes the company's address, history, sales volume, number of employees, corporate family affiliations, parent or subsidiary relationships, headquarters and branch locations, and names and titles of executives.

Available through such vendors as DIALOG.

Donnelley Demographics

On-line data base that provides demographic data from the U.S. Census Bureau. It also provides its own related current-year and five-year projections. Data can be searched, segmented, and presented in many ways. These range from the most broad, such as the United States in total, to increasingly smaller areas such as state, county, city, town, and zip code area. Additional ways for searching, segmenting, and presenting these data include metropolitan statistical areas (MSAs), areas of dominant influence (ADIs), and A. C. Nielsen's designated market areas and selling areas. Furthermore, the demographics can be separated according to age, sex, race, industry, occupation, marital status, families, mobility, households, education, housing, or income.

Available through such vendors as DIALOG.

Editor and Publisher Market Guide

Provides information about population, households, principal industries, retail sales and outlets, and so on for more than 1,500 cities in the United States and Canada (only those in which a newspaper is published). Also included are estimates of such data as population and personal income according to county, city, and designated market segment.

Updates: Annually (since 1884).

Publisher: *Editor and Publisher Magazine* (New York).

Electronic Yellow Pages

On-line data base that provides listings from nearly all the 4,800 telephone books in the United States. As a result, it contains the single largest listing of American companies available. Information can be searched, selected, and reported according to state, county, city, postal service zip code, telephone area code, size of company, size of city, type of business, or type of Yellow Page listing.

Available through such vendors as DIALOG.

FIND/SVP Reports and Studies Index

On-line data base that provides a brief description (but not a summary of findings) for over 11,000 marketing research studies done by more than five hundred research firms. It includes citations of market research reports, consumer and product studies, store audit reports, subscription research services, multiclient industry studies, and surveys of fifty-five industries worldwide. For products or topics of interest, the names of related studies, organizations that conducted the studies, contact information, and order procedures for obtaining copies of particular studies are provided. (This on-line data base corresponds with the company's annual printed publication, *FINDEX: The Directory of Market Research Reports, Studies and Surveys*).

Available through such vendors as DIALOG.

A Guide to Consumer Markets

Provides information about marketplace behavior of consumers, and includes data about population, employment, income, expenditures, and prices.

Updates: Annually.

Publisher: The Conference Board (New York).

Index of Patents Issued from the U.S. Patent Office

Provides information about patents in two volumes. An index of the government's *Official Gazette* is presented in Volume 1. This information includes the names of individuals who received a patent during the year, a description of the invention, and the patent number, issue date, and classification. An index of patents according to the subject of invention number, as indicated by the *Manual of Classification* code, is presented in Volume 2. Also in Volume 2 is a listing of depository libraries that receive the *Official Gazette*.

Updates: Annually.

Publisher: Patent Office (Washington, DC).

Index of Trademarks Issued from the U.S. Patent Office

Provides information about trademarks issued or published in the *Official Gazette* during the year. The information is organized alphabetically according to those who registered a trademark.

Updates: Annually.

Publisher: Patent Office (Washington, DC).

International Directory of the American Marketing Association and Marketing Services Guide

Provides information about American Marketing Association membership worldwide, and organizations that provide marketing services.

Updates: Annually.

Publisher: American Marketing Association (Chicago, IL).

Journal of Marketing

Within the "Marketing Literature Review" section of each quarterly issue of the *Journal of Marketing*, information is provided in the form of an annotated bibliography about published articles pertinent to marketing. The sources of these articles are related scholarly periodicals in business, economics, and the social sciences. The information is arranged according to marketing topics.

Updates: Quarterly.

Publisher: American Marketing Association (Chicago, IL).

Management and Marketing Abstracts

On-line data base that presents bibliographic abstracts of primary interest to individuals and organizations involved in management and marketing. The information includes abstracts and summaries from over 100 international journals and a wide range of monographs, books, published conference proceedings, conference papers, newsletters, and corporate reports.

Available through such vendors as Pergamon InfoLine.

Market Guide

Provides marketing information for more than 1,500 cities that have newspapers in the United States and Canada. This information includes data about population, number of households, transportation, climate, retail outlets, principal industries, banks, automobiles, and so forth. One section of the *Market Guide* presents tables pertaining to population, personal income, households, and retail sales for metropolitan areas. As this section is similar to the information presented in the *Survey of Buying Power* (published by *Sales and Marketing Management*), combining the two sections can provide marketing researchers with a good cross-check technique to assess the accuracy of data.

Updates: Annually.

Publisher: *Editor and Publisher* (New York).

Marketing Economics Guide[1]

Provides statistical estimates for 3,100 counties in the United States, all metropolitan areas, and 1,500 U.S. cities. This guide is comprised of three parts. Part 1 provides county rankings for the various statistics in Part 2 and Part 3. Part 2 provides tables on population, households, and disposable income. Part 3 provides estimates about retail sales.

Updates: Annually.

Publisher: Marketing Economics Institute (Jamaica Estates, NY). Available in printed, looseleaf format.

Marketing Information Guide

Provides information in the form of annotated summaries for current publications and reports that involve government data relevant to marketing and distribution.

Updates: Monthly.

Publisher: U.S. Department of Commerce (Washington, DC).

MRI Business-to-Business

On-line data base that provides the results of surveys, by Mediamark Research, pertaining to what products (and services) that businesses purchases for their own use. The information includes the results of interviews conducted annually with about 4,000 professionals and managers. With a focus on business products and magazines, thirty-five product categories are assessed (including office equipment, advertising, and banking services) and the professional audience for over 200 magazines is measured. Also included are the respondents' demographics (and occupation), type of company, and company size.

Available through such vendors as Interactive Market Systems, Telmar Group, and MSA.

MRI National Study

On-line data base that provides the results of a semiannual survey conducted by Mediamark Research. These surveys question about 20,000 American adults about their television viewing, radio listening, and magazine reading. Information about the respondents' consumer behavior is included, as well as their demographics. The data base comprises over 200 specific magazines, and includes where the magazines are read, the length of time they are read, and subseuent actions such as buying an advertised product or using a published recipe.

Available through such vendors as Interactive Market Systems, Telmar Group, and MSA.

MRI 10 Mediamarkets

On-line data base that provides media and marketing information on ten major markets: Boston, Chicago, Cleveland, Detroit, Los Angeles, New York, Philadelphia, San Francisco, St. Louis, and Washington, DC This information includes audience estimates for respective newspapers, radio stations, and television news programs. Also included are the respondents' demographics and usage patterns for many products and brand names.

Available through such vendors as Interactive Market Systems, Telmar Group, and MSA.

PTS MARS (Predicasts' Marketing and Advertising Reference Service)

On-line data base that contains over 30,000 citations on marketing of consumer products and services. Citations include abstracts from over 110 publications which include magazines, newsletters, trade publications, journals, and relevant sections of major U.S. newspapers. Searches can be done by Predicasts' product codes, American government Standard Industrial Classification (SIC Codes), geographical location, or by information included in the abstracts.

Updates: Periodically, but frequently.

Available through such vendors as DIALOG.

PTS PROMPT (Predicasts' Overview of Markets and Technology)

On-line data base regarding new products, acquisitions, marketing, finance, foreign trade, market size, market share, and manufacturing for virtually all industries and products. Information includes company, product, and market information. The data base provides worldwide citations, with abstracts, on over 1,200 business periodicals and magazines, of which more than 200 publications are from outside the United States. This data base also provides citations from sources such as analysis reports issued by brokerage houses, research studies, and government publications.

Updates: Weekly.

Available through such vendors as BRS, Data-Star, DIALOG, and VU/TEXT. Also available from the company on CD-ROM.

Rand McNally Commercial Atlas and Marketing Guide

Provides various marketing information that includes data about population, auto registrations, and so forth. Also included are data from the *Survey of Buying Power*, such as information about retail sales. A central aspect of this guide are the annotated maps for approximately 100,000 geographical areas in the United States. These areas include states, cities, towns, metropolitan areas, trading areas, MSAs, zip codes areas, etc.

Updates: Annually. It was published in its 122th edition in 1991.

Publisher: The Rand McNally Company (Chicago, IL). Toll-free telephone number within the United States: 800-284-6565.

Sourcebook of County Demographics

This information is analogous to the *Sourcebook of Zip Code Demographics*. A primary difference is that the respective information is provided according to counties in the United States.

Updates: Annually.

Publisher: CACI Marketing System (Fairfax, VA).

The Sourcebook of Zip Code Demographics

Information in this book is organized according to zip code areas in the United States. Both government census data and proprietary marketing data are provided. Included in this information are estimates for population and housing (including number of households and housing profile), demographic figures (percentage by age distribution, race, and median age), socioeconomic data (median household income, education, employment profile), income and buying power (percentage distribution of households according to income level). Also included is a purchasing potential index according to types of stores and in regard to savings, loans, and investments.

Updates: Annually. It was published in its seventh edition in 1992.

Publisher: CACI Marketing Systems (Fairfax, VA) and distributed by Gale Research (Detroit, MI). Toll-free telephone number within the United States: 800-877-4253.

Standard Rate and Data Service

Provides information on rates and related information for advertising media, and is recognized as the standard source for estimating expenses related to advertising. Included in this information are current advertising rates and related information related to television stations, radio stations, magazines, business publications, newspapers, films, transportation-related media, and other media in the United States, Canada, and Mexico. Some additional marketing information is provided on a limited basis.

This company provides a wide variety of descriptively titled publications. These, for example, include: *Business Publications and Rates, Canadian Advertising Rates and Data, Community Publication Rates and Data, Consumer Magazine and Farm Publication Rates and Data, Co-Op Service Directory, Direct Mail List Rates and Data, Network Rates and Data, Newspaper Rates and Data, Print Media Production Data, SRDS Newspaper Circulation Analysis, Sport Radio Rates and Data*, and *Transit Advertising Rates and Data*. The company also provides international editions, that provide similar information for countries that include England, France, Italy, Mexico, and West Germany.

Updates: Varies, with most information updated monthly, while some is quarterly and semiannually.

Publisher: Standard Rate and Data Service (Skokie, IL).

Statistics of Communications Common Carriers

Provides information about all companies in the United States in the telephone, telegraph, and communications businesses and involved in interstate or foreign communications. This source of secondary data is especially valuable for marketing research projects involving particular utilities, as well as for the communications industry in general.

Updates: Annually.

Publisher: U.S. Federal Communications Commission (Washington, DC).

Study of Media and Markets

On-line data base that provides the results of the Simmons Market Research Bureau's annual survey of about 19,000 American adults. This survey concerns the respondents' use of about 4,000 brands of products in over 800 product categories. The current data base has over 2 million pieces of information which includes audience measures about magazines, television, radio, newspapers, outdoor advertising, and the Yellow Pages. These measures include both demographic and psychographic information. There are twenty-seven demographic categories which include age, sex, income, education, occupation, marital status, number of children, geographic region, and value of residence. These data can be combined with other data base information such as PRIZM (the Claritas company product, *Potential Ratings for Zip Markets*) and VALS (the Stanford Research Institute values and life-styles study).

Available through such vendors as Simmons Market Research Bureau and Interactive Market Systems.

SuperSite

On-line data base by CACI, Inc., combines past census data (1960, 1970, 1980, 1990) with current-year updates and five-year forecasts. CACI can provide demographic descriptions, sales potential estimates, or ACORN (A Classification Of Residential Neighborhoods) profiles for almost any geographical area in the United States. Such demographic information as population, income, prices of housing, occupation, automobiles, educational attainment, family composition, and household appliances can be provided for more than 60,000 census tracts and minor civil divisions. Furthermore, sales potential estimates are available for 165 lines of retail merchandise, 16 types of retail outlets, and 3 types of banking services.

ACORN is a related on-line data base product which provides U.S. census information according to one of forty-four market segments. Each market segment include a profile in terms of type of neighborhood's demographics, economy, and housing.

Available through such vendors as CompuServe and Chase Econometrics.

Survey of Buying Power[2]

Survey of Buying Power is reported in the form of additional issues in August and November of each year of the *Sales and Marketing Management* magazine. It provides information about population, income, and retail sales, categorized according to geographical areas.

There are two parts to the *Survey of Buying Power*. Part 1, which is the August issue, provides current statistical estimates for population according to age group, households, effective buying income, and retail sales for six categories of stores. This information is provided for all U.S. states, counties, metropolitan areas, and some cities.

Part 2, which is the November issue, provides several different types of information. For example, one type provides projections, in terms of percentage changes over the next five years, of markets in various metropolitan areas. These projections include population, effective buying income, and retail sales. Another type of information provides profiles of so-called television and newspaper markets. Again, these profiles are expressed in terms of population, effective buying income, and retail sales. A third type of information provides a ranking of metropolitan areas according to retail sales for each of ten merchandise lines.

Updates: Annually.

Published by *Sales and Marketing Management* (New York).

Additional Related Sources

The *Survey of Buying Power*, as published by *Sales and Marketing Management*, involves additional sources of secondary data of value to marketing researchers. There are at least three such publications:

Survey of Buying Power: Canadian Data—This publication provides the standard *Survey of Buying Power* information but does so according to provinces, counties, and cities in Canada.

Survey of Industrial Commercial Buying Power—This publication is an extra issue of *Sales and Marketing Management* that is published in April of each year. It provides information according to counties in the United States. Included in this information are data bout the number of industrial establishments, the number with over 100 employees, and the number according to four-digit SIC codes for counties with at least 2,000 employees.

Survey of Selling Costs—This publication is an extra issue of *Sales and Marketing Management* that is published in February of each year. It provides selling cost data and "Metro Market Profiles" for 100 of the largest metropolitan markets in the United States and six of the largest metropolitan markets in Canada.

Survey of World Advertising Expenditures

Provides information about the expenditures spent on advertising around the world. The information is categorized according to media and country.

Updates: Annually.

Publisher: Starch, INRA, Hooper (New York).

Trademarkscan

On-line data base that contains all the active registered and pending trademarks on file with the U.S. Patent and Trademark Office. The inactive trademarks since 1983 are included. There is together, a total of over 800,000 records with about 1,500 weekly additions. Information provided includes a full description of the goods or services, a registration number and data, current status, and the owner's name and address for each trademark.

Updates: Weekly.

Available through such vendors as DIALOG.

VALS/MRI

On-line data base that classifies survey respondents' into the nine VALS (Values And Life-Styles) types developed by the Stanford Research Institute. Based on their attitudes, wants, and beliefs, American consumers are grouped into three categories: need-driven, outer-directed, and inner-directed. These categories are then subdivided into the nine VALS types, each of which has distinct buying styles, media use patterns, and demography.

Available through such vendors as Interactive Market Systems and Telmar Group.

NOTES

1. There are some important similarities and differences between the *Marketing Economics Guide* and the *Survey of Buying Power* published by *Sales and Marketing Management*. Most important, parts of these two publications are similar enough to cross-check secondary data accuracy in some instances. However, since the two publications are not identical, it is not possible to cross-check all data. Nonetheless, because of these differences, the two publications together provide a valuable resource when a marketing research project calls for different geographical categorizations for reporting populations, households, disposable personal income, and retail sales.

The *Survey of Buying Power* and the *Marketing Economics Guide* are, first of all, both annual publications with substantial value to marketing researchers. While the *Survey*, is more of a traditional, or established, source of secondary data, the *Guide* serves as an important complement. For example, consider the following comparisons of population, income, and retail sales.

Population: The *Survey* (part 1) provides population by age group for each geographical area. The *Guide* does not provide population data by any age group. However, unlike the *Survey*, the *Guide* does provide the percentage of urban and black populations. It also provides the number of households according to eight income group sizes, while the *Survey* covers only four such groups.

Income: The reporting of disposable income is similar, with the *Survey*'s information describing effective buying income and the *Guide*'s information concerning disposable personal income.

Retail Sales: The *Survey* reports estimated retail sales according to six retail store categories, while the *Guide* does so according to nine categories. Furthermore, for each category, the *Guide* reports retail sales information for several more cities than does the *Survey*. Depending on the focus of a particular marketing research project, these additional cities may make the *Guide* more valuable.

2. See note 1.

8

Global/Worldwide
Information Sources

There are data bases and sources of secondary data specific to almost
every country in the world. To locate these, the reader is referred to
the respective directories of data bases (computer and printed).
Sections of these data bases are clearly designated to easily locate
information about a specific country or region of the world. What
follows here is only a sample (albeit an important sample for
marketing and marketing research).

Many secondary data sources and almost all data bases access
information that is not restricted to any one geographical region or
country. For example, even an American data base that focuses on
information pertaining to the United States will include some refer-
ences to information pertaining to other countries.

Most of the items in this chapter pertain to multiple countries
around the world. Although they must necessarily be located in some
country, their information generally pertains to more than a single
region or country of the world. There is one exception: in a few
instances, data bases specific to a particular world region and its
leading country are presented and so designated: Europe led by
Germany, Asia led by Japan, and the Americas led by the United
States. The reason for selecting these three countries is because they
are currently the most economically and politically powerful in the
world and in their respective regions of the world.

Because the majority of this book part (Chapters 7 through 11) pertains most directly to American secondary data sources about the United States, a respective, separate listing of secondary data sources (analogous to Germany and Japan) is not provided in this chapter for the United States. However, at the same time, the reader should be aware that many of the so-called "American" sources (printed and computer) have counterparts in England, Canada, and elsewhere. (One such example is Trademarkscan.)   Other specific secondary data sources with significant information relevant to countries other than the United States, and which are listed in Part 2 of this book but *not* within this chapter include:

ABI/Inform

Advertising Age: Foreign Agency Income Reports

American Statistics Index: Index to International Statistics

Broadcasting

Business Periodicals Index

Commodity Year Book

Dissertation Abstracts International

Editor and Publisher Market Guide

Encyclopedia of Associations: International Organizations (Volume 4)

Encyclopedia of Geographic Information Sources (international volume)

Federal Reserve Bulletin

The Fortune International 500

Greenbook: International Directory of Marketing Research Companies and Services

Guide to Industrial Statistics

Highlights of U.S. Export and Import Trade

International Directories in Print

International Directory of the American Marketing Association and Marketing Services Guide

International Directories in Print

International Directory of Corporate Affiliations

Investext

Management and Marketing Abstracts

Market Guide

Predicasts Forecasts

PTS Prompt (Predicasts' Overview of Markets and Technology)

Public Affairs Information Service Bulletin: PAIS International

SilverPlatter

Standard & Poor's Corporate Records

Standard & Poor's Register of Corporations, Directors, and Executives

Standard Directory of Worldwide Marketing

Standard Rate and Data Service (international editions)

Statistics of Communications Common Carriers

Survey of Buying Power: Canadian Data

Survey of Current Business

Survey of Selling Costs

Survey of World Advertising Expenditures

The Wall Street Journal: Dow Jones News Services

INTERNATIONAL INFORMATION

Asian Profiles

On-line data base that provides purchasing data for adults aged twenty-five years or older in seven Asian cities: Bangkok, Hong

Kong, Jakarta, Kuala Lumpur, Manila, Singapore, and Taipei.

Language: English

Updates: Every three years.

Vendor: Available through vendors such as Interactive Market Systems. Also available on CD-ROM.

Directory of European Databases and Databanks

This directory is available in printed format and as an on-line data base. The on-line format, known as ECHO (for European Community Host Organisation), presents the most up-to-date version of the printed format. To access the on-line version, the user does not have to be registered. Furthermore, instructions are in eight languages: Danish, Dutch, English, French, German, Italian, Portuguese, and Spanish. The directory and companion on-line data base provides the following information:

Subject Index of the Data Bases and Data Banks (with several hundred entries),

Alphabetical List of Data Bases and Data Banks with Summary of Contents (with over a thousand data bases and data banks listed),

List of Data Bases Per Host,

List of Hosts, and

List of Postal, Telegraph, and Telephone Authority (PTT) Contact Points. [1]

For information, address correspondence to ECHO (the European Community Host Organisation), B.P. 2372, L-1023; Luxembourg. Telephone: 352-48-80-41; Telex: 2181; Telefax: 352-48-80-40.

Directory of Public Data Bases: European Communities

This is not an on-line data base but a directory of on-line data bases. It identifies fifty data bases produced by the Commission of the European Communities. The intent is to update the directory regularly. These data bases focus on information about countries in the European Communities. All are in English, while some are in all nine languages of the European Community: Danish, Dutch, English, French, German, Greek, Italian, Portuguese, and Spanish. The directory provides the following information:

Index by Name of Data Base—(e.g., Abel, Agrep, Eurocontact, Euristote, INFO 92, etc.).

Index by Type of Data Base—(1) bibliographical data bases, (2) mixed bibliographical/factual data bases, (3) factual data bases, and (4) statistical data bases.

Index by Subject of Data Base—(1) documentation and information market, (2) science, environment and health, (3) technology, (4) law, (5) business and economics, and (6) agriculture.

Description of Data bases—Full name, contents, type of data base, producer, geographical coverage, language of data stored, data base size, time span, updating, tapes/diskettes, microfiche availability, listings, corresponding publications, information service/datashop, distribution, on-line distributor(s), products offered, software used, downloading facilities, off-line distributor(s), products offered.

List of Host and Distribution Organizations—Names, addresses, and telephone numbers are provided for all organizations, with telex and fax numbers also included for many of the organizations.

For information, address correspondence to Mr. A. Berger, Computing Centre; 200 rue de la Loi, ARL 3/4, B-1049, Brussels, Belgium.

Europa World Year Book

Information is provided in two volumes according to country. This book includes information about the respective country's recent history, economy, government, political organizations, and holidays. The information also includes the names of the most important newspapers, periodicals, television stations, radio stations, banks, insurance companies, trade associations, and railroads. In addition, at the front of the first volume, there is information regarding some international organizations.

Updates: Annually.

Publisher: Europa Publications (London).

European Directory of Marketing Information Sources

For specific countries, information is provided about official government publications (including statistical publications), libraries and information sources, leading market research companies, information data bases, abstracts and indexes, major business and marketing journals, leading business and marketing associations, and European business contacts such as embassies and chambers of commerce.

Updates: It was published in its second edition in 1991; its first edition was in 1987.

Publisher: Euromonitor Publications (London). Telephone: 01-251-8024.

European Marketing Data

Provides comparative country statistics on marketing topics and on basic economic indicators for thirty-three countries. The marketing information includes data about retail sales according to type, advertising patterns, media (including number of televisions and radios), and consumption of various consumer products. This information includes comparisons between countries in Western Europe and Eastern Europe. The economic information includes data about population, households, consumer expenditures, consumer prices, market sizes in particular industries, transportation, and retailing. The sources from which these data are obtained sources are described at the front of the publication.

Updates: Annually.

Publisher: Euromonitor (London).

Exporters' Encyclopedia

Provides detailed information about shipments made to every country in the world. Included in this information are types of transportation available and used, regulations, types of communication, trade organizations foreign to the United States, export information, and listings of ports.
Updates: Annually.
Publisher: Dun & Bradstreet (New York).

Export Publications Catalogue

This publication provides details of export-related publications written jointly by the commercial staff of the Foreign and Commonwealth Office based overseas and Department for Enterprise export staff. Separate indexes are provided by country and product section.
All the major countries of the world are covered by these publications. The publications provide background information on the country, its commerce, detailed reports on selected product sectors of those countries, and advice for exporting.
For information, address correspondence to DTI Export Publications, P.O. Box 55, Stratford-upon-Avon, Warwickshire, CV37 9GE, England. Telephone: 0789-296212.

Foreign Commerce Handbook: Basic Information and Guide to Sources

Provides information, as its title states, for information sources pertaining to business in countries other than the United States.
Updates: Every five years.
Publisher: U.S. Chamber of Commerce (Washington, DC).

Foreign Economic Trends and Their Implications for the United States

Provides information in pamphlet form about the economic trends and their possible implications for trade within and between the

United States. The information is prepared by embassies and other personnel associated with the U.S. Foreign Service.

Updates: Annually (and, in some cases, semiannually) for each country.

Publisher: U.S. Bureau of International Commerce (Washington, DC).

German Business Scope

On-line data base that provides trade, sales, and distribution information pertaining to Germany.

Language: English.

Updates: Daily.

Vendor: Available through vendors such as CORIS, Data-Star, and DIALOG.

German Economic Outlook

On-line data base with over three thousand ratings on the economic outlook for Germany from surveys of German businesses.

Language: English.

Updates: Monthly.

Vendor: Available through vendors such as DRI/McGraw-Hill, Information Plus, and Reuters Information Services.

German Macroeconomic

On-line data base with about 23,000 time series of German macroeconomic data such as production, money supply, orders, and inventories. Also includes industry-specific data.

Language: English.

Updates: Monthly.

Vendor: Available through vendors such as the WEFA Group on an ongoing subscription basis, or through Dimensions on a per-use basis.

German Statistical Data

On-line data base with over 60,000 time series on economic and demographic data on Germany.
Language: English.
Updates: Monthly.
Vendor: Available through vendors such as DRI/McGraw-Hill and Data Products Division.

Index to International Statistics

This index is related to the *American Statistics Index*, and provides abstracts and indexes for the statistical publications of major international government organizations, such as the United Nations and the Organization for Economic Cooperation and Development. The *Index to International Statistics* identifies data about individual countries, but it does not provide names of publications for each country.
Updates: Monthly (with annual culminations).
Publisher: U.S. Congressional Information Service (Bethesda, MD).

International Business Clearinghouse

On-line data base that serves as a worldwide bartering and brokerage service. It provides a comprehensive listing of products and services offered for sale or trade by companies around the world. Information pertains to a variety of business enterprises that include media, computer companies, manufacturers, distributors, and service companies such as airlines and hotels.
Available through such vendors as Western Union FYI, ITF, and NewsNet.

International Directory of Marketing Information Sources

Provides the same types of information as the *European Directory of Marketing Information Sources*, but it does so for countries other than European countries. Therefore, for a more complete description of this secondary data source, see the *European Directory of Marketing Information Sources* (earlier in this chapter). However, the same precautionary note is appropriate here in regard to the date of the material: although the publication is an excellent source of information, it is extremely dated, and unless a more recent edition is published, in its 1988 version it is likely to be of only marginal value to marketing researchers.

Publisher: Euromonitor Publications (London).

Japan Consumer Electronics Scan

On-line data base on electronic products, their prices, availability, and target markets.

Language: English.

Updates: Daily.

Vendor: Available through vendors such as CORIS, Data-Star, and DIALOG.

Japan Economic Daily

On-line data base on Japanese business, industry, economics and finance.

Language: English.

Updates: Daily.

Vendor: Available through vendors such as Data-Star, Dow Jones and Company, Dow Jones News/Retrieval, and Delphi.

Japan Report: Product Opportunities

On-line data base about Japanese products and technologies available for licensing, distribution, and other business relationships.

Language: English.

Updates: Daily.

Vendor: Available through vendors such as Thomson Financial Networks, CORIS, and DIALOG.

Moody's International Manual

Provides financial information (in two volumes) pertaining to major corporations in about 100 countries. The information is organized according to country. Information provided for each country, typically includes a brief financial history, description of business and property, names of officers, and financial statement data. In addition, the center (blue-color) pages contain comparative international data.

Updates: Annually (with intermittent supplements).

Publisher: Moody's Investors Service (New York).

National Trade Data Bank (NTDB)

The National Trade Data Bank is a collection of trade reports and statistical data from eleven different U.S. government agencies. The information embodies well over 100,000 pages of data focused on helping American companies export their products. This information is provided in CD-ROM format.

Information can be obtained in a number of ways. For example, in addition to purchasing the CD-ROM, key words (such as housewares in Japan) can be faxed to NTDB. NTDB will perform the search and send by return fax the titles of the documents located under those key words and the charge by item. The interested person can return the form with the desired documents marked and appropriate payment. The documents will be copied and returned in almost any requested format: mail, fax, diskette (either 5 1/4 inch or 3 1/2 inch, a variety of standard word processing formats, or in ASCII).

The user fee charged for obtaining information from NTDB is rather small and is kept to a minimum while still covering costs associated with copying and searching for the data.

These data include macroeconomic reporting on the balance of trade, census statistics on imports and exports, many market research reports prepared by U.S. embassies from around the world, and over 4,000 marketing research reports that pertain to sales opportunities in nearly 100 countries. These marketing research reports range from complete "industry subsector analysis reports," containing ten to thirty pages of information on a market sector in a specific country, to "international market intelligence reports," which are shorter and focus on sales opportunities for specific products in one market.

For information, address correspondence to Anita Chan, U.S. and Foreign Commercial Service, American Consulate General in Hong Kong, 26 Garden Road, Hong Kong. Telephone: 852-521-1467; Fax: 852-845-9800.

Overseas Business Reports

Provides information obtained from the U.S. Office of International Marketing. The information involves the market potential, trade regulations, business practices and policies, economic structure, and investment laws of various countries other than the United States Its purpose is to help businesses in the United States to access and increase their share of foreign markets.

Updates: Annually.

Publisher: U.S. Bureau of International Commerce (Washington, DC).

Political Risk Yearbook

This publication is a seven-volume series intended to be of value to both students and researchers around the world. Its focus is to gather information about governments through the world and to analyze their policy-making processes. Much of the basic information used in preparing this yearbook is provided by approximately 250 country specialists around the world.

The yearbook is comprised of a report on each country. There are individual reports on eighty-five countries that are monitored on a year-round basis. These countries are divided into seven volumes as follows:

Volume 1—North and Central America
(thirteen countries)

Volume 2—Middle East and North Africa
(thirteen countries)

Volume 3—South America (nine countries)

Volume 4—Sub-Saharan Africa (eleven countries)

Volume 5—Asia and the Pacific (sixteen countries)

Volume 6—Europe: Countries of the European Community (eleven countries)

Volume 7—Europe: Outside the European Community (twelve countries)

Each report includes at least eleven sections: (1) an extensive executive summary, (2) territory and maritime disputes, (3) fact sheets pertaining to political, government, social, and economic data for twelve key indicators, (4) background, (5) political actors, (6) regime stability, (7) turmoil, (8) international investment restrictions, (9) trade restrictions, (10) economic policies, and (11) five-year political and economic forecasts. Also included in many of the reports is an updates section.

For information, address correspondence to Customer Services, Political Risk Services, P.O. Box 6482, 222 Teall Avenue, Suite 200, Syracuse, New York 13217-6482. Telephone: 315-472-1224, Fax: 315-472-1235.

Primary International Businesses

Provides information for approximately 50,000 leading companies in 140 countries. The information is organized according to country. Also, indexes are provided according to SIC industries and company.
Updates: Annually.
Publisher: Dun's Marketing Services (New York).

Standard Directory of Worldwide Marketing

Provides information about large companies, and large advertising agencies, located outside the United states. For each company, this information provides the names of sales personnel, the name of the company's advertising agency, the approximate advertising budget, and the media used.

Updates: Annually.
Publisher: National Register Publishing Company (Wilmette, IL).

Statistical Yearbook

Provides information in the form of statistical tables, according to country, for education (including educational expenditures); science and technology; and culture and communications (including libraries, book production, periodicals including newspapers, museums, film, and broadcasting via television and radio).
Updates: Annually.
Publisher: United Nations Educational, Scientific and Cultural Organization (Paris).

Statistics and International Marketing Data and Statistics

Provides the same types of information as the *European Marketing Data* publication, except it does so for over 150 countries. For a more complete description of this secondary data source, see *European Marketing Data* (earlier in this chapter).
Updates: Annually.
Publisher: Euromonitor (London).

United Nations Demographic Yearbook

Provides detailed demographic characteristics of the population in over 200 countries. The information includes births, deaths, marriages, and divorces.
Updates: Annually.
Publisher: United Nations (New York).

United Nations Statistical Yearbook

For each country in the United Nations, information on the following topics is provided: population, work force, employment, wages, finance, education, foreign trade, transportation, communication, tourism, forestry, manufacturing, consumption, and other basic economic activities. Other related publications by the United Nations include the following:

Industrial Statistics Yearbook (Two Volumes)

Provides general information about industrial and commodity production.

International Trade Statistics Yearbook (Two Volumes)

Provides information about imports and exports according to country. This information also includes imports and exports for each country and according to commodity.

Monthly Bulletin of Statistics

Provides the same information as the *Statistical Yearbook*, but does so on a monthly basis and in a less comprehensive manner.

National Accounts Statistics (Three Volumes)

Provides information about income, gross domestic product, and consumer expenditures statistics for about 150 countries.
Updates: Annually.
Publisher: United Nations (New York).

Where to Find Business Information: A Worldwide Guide for Everyone Who Needs the Answers to Business Questions

Provides information on over 5,000 books, periodicals, and data bases. The information is organized according to subject, title, and publisher.
Updates: The reader is referred to the latest edition of this book by authors David M. Brownstone and Gorton Carruth which was published in a second edition in 1982.
Publisher: John Wiley and Sons Publishers (New York).

World Almanac and Book of Facts

Provides facts on many diverse subjects, including but certainly not limited to: politics, social issues, religious, finance, and industry.
Updates: Annually.
Publisher: Newspaper Enterprise Association (New York).

Worldcasts

Similar to *Predicasts Forecasts*, this publication provides both short- and long-range statistical forecasts for products and industries in countries other than the United States. The *Worldcasts* publication is actually comprised of four volumes pertaining to products (*World—Product-Casts*) and four volumes pertaining to regions (*World—Region al-Casts*). Information for *Worldcasts* is obtained from more than 800 publications.

Predicasts publishes several other relevant global data bases. These are *Predicasts F&S Index Europe* (which focuses on Europe) and *Predicasts F&S Index International* (which focuses on countries in the world other than Europe and the United States). These are analogous to the company's data bases that are published with a focus on the United States. Therefore, the reader is referred to the more complete discussion of *Predicasts F&S Index United States* elsewhere in Chapter 10. Note that all three of these data bases (Europe, International, and United States) are available on the on-line data base, PTS F&S Index.

Publisher: Predicasts (Cleveland). Available in print form and as an on-line data base known as *PTS Forecasts*.

Worldscope: Industrial Company Profiles

Provides concise (one-page) statistical profiles for more than 3,000 leading industrial companies in twenty-four countries and covering eighteen industries. Statistics are usually for a six-year period and include financial statement data, financial ratios, growth rate, per-share data, and similar information.

The information is collected by the Center for International

Financial Analysis in Princeton, NJ. It then is housed in the center's
WORLDSCOPE data base.

Updates: Quarterly.

Publisher: Wright Investors' Service (Bridgeport, CT). Available
in five printed, looseleaf volumes.

NOTE

1. PTT is the particular national authority in overall command of
postal and telecommunication services within a particular country. In
the United Kingdom, the General Post Office was the PTT, until it
was replaced by two other entities: The Post Office (PO) and British
Telecom (BT). In the United States there is no corresponding
organization, office, or agency. However, these matters in the United
States are regulated by the Federal Communications Commission
(FCC). See Phil Brown, *Electronics and Computer Acronyms*
(London: Butterworths, 1988), p. 200.

9

Sources of Information Regarding American Census Data and Reference Guides

Two categories of secondary data sources are presented in this chapter: American Census Data Information and reference guides.

AMERICAN CENSUS DATA INFORMATION

All the following census items are published by the Government Printing Office for the U.S. Bureau of the Census, unless specifically designated otherwise. The first two items listed here (CENDATA and *Census Catalog and Guide*) are probably the two most important items since they provide knowledge and access to the rest of the census information.

CENDATA

On-line data base service that provides access to much of the American government's census information. Availability and access to this data base is provided in the *Census Catalog and Guide* (published by the U.S. Bureau of Census; see next entry).

Updates: Annually (with intermittent updates).

Census Catalog and Guide

Publication that provides help for using the U.S. Bureau of Census information. Included in this information is a descriptive guide to census statistics and reports arranged according to census subjects (such as business and population). Also included are special tabulations and information about on-line data files (many of which are available as an on-line data base known as CENDATA; see previous entry). It comes complete with a listing of telephone numbers for contacting Census Bureau specialists by their area of expertise. The guide includes order information for all the Census Bureau's products, such as on-line data bases, computer tapes, computer diskettes, reports, maps, and microfiche.
Updates: Annually.

Census Data Index

Provides information, in the form of an index, to the Census Bureau's data, publications, and unpublished materials. Included are sections for publications, data files, and special tabulations.
Updates: Quarterly (with monthly supplements and annual culminations).

Census of Agriculture

Provides data about the number, types, and sizes of farms, land use, related employment, products, and value of products. Information is presented according to state and county. This census is supplemented by numerous other publications and bulletins published by the Department of Agriculture.
Updates: A new census of agriculture is taken every five years, in years that end in 2 and 7. However, before 1982 the updates were taken in the years ending in 4 and 9. In addition, two annual updates to these census data are *Agricultural Statistics*, published by the U.S. Department of Agriculture (Washington, DC), and the *Knight-Ridder CRB Commodity Yearbook*, published by the Commodity Research Bureau (Chicago, IL) and Knight-Ridder Financial Publishing (New

York). A third, related, annual publication is the *Knight-Ridder CRB Commodity Yearbook Statistical Supplement*.

Census of Business

This census pertains to the retail, wholesale, and selected service industries in the United States, Guam, and Virgin Islands. There are three components of the Census of Business: Census of Retail Trade, Census of Service Industries, and Census of Wholesale Trade. Related information is contained in a series of ongoing publications: *Monthly Retail Trade, Selected Service Receipts*, and *Monthly Wholesale Trade*.

Updates: A new census is taken every five years, in years ending in 2 and 7. Each of the three components are updated accordingly.

Census of Retail Trade

Provides information about sales, payroll, employees, number of establishments, sales by merchandise lines, etc., arranged by Standard Industrial Classification System code number (SIC Codes). The information is organized according to states, counties, and other areas such as Primary Metropolitan Statistical Areas (PMSAs), Consolidated Metropolitan Statistical Areas (CMSAs), and Metropolitan Statistical Areas (MSAs). Related, current data based on an annual sample survey are provided in *Monthly Retail Sales and Inventories*.

Census of Service Industries. Provides information about retail service organizations such as hotels, beauty parlors, and laundries and does so in terms of receipts, employment, number of units, payrolls, and so forth. However, no information is provided in this census for the real estate industry, insurance industry, or the various service professions such as dentist, lawyer, or physicians. The information is organized according to states, Standard Metropolitan Statistical Areas (SMSAs), counties, and cities. Current, related data are provided in the government's *Monthly Selected Services Receipts* publication and *Service Annual Survey*.

Census of Wholesale Trade. Provides information about sales, number of establishments, payrolls, warehouse space, expenses, and so forth, arranged by SIC code number. The information is organized according to states, SMSAs, and counties. Related, current data based on an annual sample survey are provided in *Monthly Wholesale Trade: Sales and Inventories.*

Census of Construction Industries

Provides information on the value of inventories, assets, and employment for businesses involved in contract construction, construction of property for sale, and in subdividing real property into smaller divisions. The information reported is organized according to states.

Updates: A new census is taken every five years, in years ending in 2 and 7.

Census of Government

Provides information on general characteristics of state and local governments: employment, payroll size, indebtedness, revenues, expenses, and so on.

Updates: A new census is taken every five years, in years ending in 2 and 7.

Census of Housing

Provides data according to states, counties, MSAs, and cities. Through the use of several volumes, the collective information includes details about housing conditions and occupancy statistics.

Volume 1—Characteristics of Housing Units. It includes cost of housing, monthly rent, average value, type of structure, size, condition of building, year built, occupancy figures, water and sewer facilities, financial characteristics, average number of rooms, occupancy by nonwhites, and equipment (such as washers, stoves, and air conditioning).

Volume 2—Metropolitan Housing Characteristics.

Volume 3 — Subject Reports.

Volume 4 — Components of Inventory Change.

Volume 5 — Residential Finance.

Updates: A new census is taken every ten years, in years ending in 0 in conjunction with the *Census of Population* in the United States. Between census years, the census of housing is supplemented with the annual *American Housing Survey* which provides information about housing characteristics, neighborhood quality, financial characteristics, and so forth (in the biennial *Housing-150* publication), and other similar data for eleven selected metropolitan areas (in the *Housing-170* publication). Another supplement (*Current Housing Reports*) provides annual and quarterly update data on topics such as housing vacancies, home ownership, apartment space, and characteristics of apartments completed.

Census of Manufacturers

Provides information about capital expenditures, value added, payrolls, employment, number of establishments, inventories, and so on. This information is provided according to different manufacturing industries as grouped into nearly 500 classes. Two related reports are the *Final Area Reports* (which presents data according to geographic region) and *Final Industry Reports* (which presents data according to type of industry).

Updates: A new census is taken every five years, in years ending in 2 and 7. Between each census, update information is provided in the *Annual Survey of Manufactures*. In addition, the *Current Industrial Reports* present information on the monthly and annual production figures for selected commodities.

Census of Mineral Industries

Provides information on characteristics of the mining industry: employment, payroll, cost of supplies, number of operations, businesses, production volume, value of shipments, capital expenditure, equipment, water use, and so forth.

For related information, the U.S. Bureau of Mines (U.S. Department of the Interior) publishes an annual *Minerals Yearbook*. While similar information is provided, the two sources differ in their categorization of the data: the *Census of Mineral Industries* categorizes information according to an "industrial classification" and the *Minerals Yearbook* uses a "product classification" system.

Updates: A new census is taken every five years, in years ending in 2 and 7.

Census of Population

Provides information about population characteristics according to states, counties, MSAs, urbanized areas, and census tracts. Information includes demographics such as age, sex, race, marital status, family composition, national origin, citizenship status, employment, income, level of education, and other characteristics.

Updates: A new census is taken every ten years, in years ending in 0.

Census of Transportation

Provides information on truck inventory, truck use, bus inventory, bus use, truck and bus miles, transportation of commodities and so on. This information is generally not publicly available elsewhere, so the Census of Transportation is the most important source for such American transportation data.

Updates: A new census is taken every five years, in years ending with 2 and 7.

Current Population Reports

Current Population Reports are extracted from the Census of Population. Therefore, updates are compiled in conjunction with the Census of Population, which is taken every ten years, in years ending in 0. These reports consist of data on topics such as population characteristics (in the *Population-20* publication), population estimates and projections (in the *Population-25* publication), and consumer income and socioeconomic characteristics of persons, families, and households (in the *Population-60* publication). Descriptions of specific reports follow.

Characteristics of the Population

Provides separate reports for the United States, each of the fifty states, District of Columbia, Puerto Rico, Guam, the Virgin Islands, American Samoa, and the Trust Territory of the Pacific Islands.

General Population Characteristics

Provides data on age, sex, race, Hispanic origin, marital status, and household relationships. This information is presented according to states, counties, MSAs, PMSAs, CMSAs, urbanized areas, county subdivisions, places of 1,000 or more inhabitants, Indian reservations, and Alaskan native villages.

General Social and Economic Characteristics

Provides data on "population subjects" (e.g., migration, education, income, etc.), as collected on a sample basis. The information is presented according to states, counties, MSAs, urbanized areas, places of 2,500 or more inhabitants, Indian reservations, and Alaskan native villages.

Number of Inhabitants

Provides the final official population counts according to states, counties, MSAs, urbanized areas, county subdivisions, incorporated places, and census-designated areas.

Population Subject Reports

Provides separate reports focusing on a particular subject such as migration, education, income, the older population, and racial and ethnic groups. Reporting of the data varies, with some reported according to national or regional level and other data reported according to states, large cities, MSAs, and Indian reservations.

Factfinder for the Nation

Provides information about the range of U.S. Bureau of Census information, their subjects, and some suggested uses.
Updates: Irregularly.
Publisher: U.S. Bureau of the Census (Washington, DC).

Guide to Industrial Statistics

Provides information about the Census Bureau's data and programs about industry in the United States. The information includes the type of data available and where they are located.
Publisher: U.S. Bureau of the Census (Washington, DC).

Guide to 1980 Census Data on the Elderly

Provides information about census publications pertaining to the elderly population.
Publisher: U.S. Bureau of the Census and U.S. Administration on Aging, 1986 (Washington, DC).

Highlights of U.S. Export and Import Trade

Provides information about international trade, organized according to type of commodity, country, region of the world, regions and districts of the United States customs, method of shipment, and category of end use. The data for this report are obtained from the

U.S. Bureau of Customs, and the report is the most comprehensive of its nature.

Updates: Monthly.

Publisher: Bureau of the Census (Washington, DC).

REFERENCE GUIDES

The items listed here are reference guides that provide more general information. However, they are at the same time specific to business and are helpful to marketing researchers involved with particular research projects.

American Statistics Index

This index serves as a comprehensive guide to the huge amount of statistical data available to the public by the American federal government. As such, it provides information about secondary data that is available from all agencies and office of the federal American government. Information is provided in the form of indexes and abstracts for statistical publications of the federal government, congressional committees, and other federal programs. Its tables are indexed by subject and category, commodity or industry, geographic area, title, and report number. There are three related guides: (1) *Statistical Reference Index*, (2) the *CIS Index*, and (3) the *Index to International Statistics*. This last index is discussed elsewhere in this book part, in regard to international or global secondary data.

The *Statistical Reference Index* serves as a complement to the *American Statistics Index*, and has a similar format. As such, it provides information about American statistical publications by nongovernment sources, including trade and professional associations, institutes, commercial publishers, businesses, independent research organizations, state governments, and university research centers. It is especially useful for identifying statistical publications of trade associations for a specific industry and annual statistical issues of trade journals.

The *CIS Index* is a monthly index and abstract that provides information which helps to identify, evaluate, and obtain information contained in the working papers of the U.S. Congress. It covers hearings, prints, documents, reports, and special publications.

Updates: Monthly updates with annual culminations.

Publisher: Congressional Information Service (Bethesda, MD). Available in printed form and as an on-line data base known as *ASI*.

Business Information Sources

Provides an annotated bibliography of books, periodicals, and reference sources according to business subject area, including specific information pertaining to marketing and marketing research. Of its twenty-one sections, three focus on business statistical sources, one on investment sources, and one on marketing, with the last including handbooks, books, and reference books on marketing, market research, product development, selling, advertising, and retailing.

Updates: The reader is referred to the latest edition of this book by author Lorna M. Daniells. It was published in its first edition in 1985 (Berkeley, CA: University of California Press), with a second edition published in 1992, and a third edition in 1993.

Encyclopedia of Business Information Sources

Identifies sources of information on approximately 1,000 subjects and industries. Included in this publication are lists of related abstracts, indexes, bibliographies, directories, on-line data bases, periodicals, statistical sources, trade associations, and professional organizations for each topic.

Publisher: Gale Research Company (Detroit, MI). The reader is referred to the latest edition.

Encyclopedia of Geographic Information Sources

In addition to listing sources of information for states and regions of the United States, the U.S. volume includes sources of information for over three-hundred cities. The international volume includes sources pertaining to seventy-five countries and more than eighty major cities outside of the United States.

Publisher: Gale Research Company (Detroit, MI). The reader is referred to the latest edition.

Monthly Catalog of United States Government Publications

Provides information about publications of the U.S. government. The information is organized according to subject, titles, and publication number (which is also according to the issuing agency).

Updates: Monthly with semiannual culminations.

Publisher: United States Government Printing Office (Washington, DC).

Standard Industrial Classification Manual

Explains the coding system developed by the federal government in regard to collecting and tabulating data on products, services, and industries. That code, as well as its expanded versions, is commonly known as the SIC code.

The SIC code is especially valuable when dealing with the government's various censuses material. This code is also used by many commercial sources such as publishers of directories, indexes, and abstracts. For marketing researchers, the SIC code (and thus this Standard Industrial Classification Manual) is helpful for identifying industry data about a particular product.

Publisher: U.S. Office of Management and Budget, in 1987 (Washington, DC).

Statistics Sources

Provides a guide to data on over 20,000 topics. The information is arranged alphabetically according to topic and geographic location. The reader is referred to the latest edition.

Updates: Annually.

Publisher: Gale Research Company (Detroit, MI).

10

Information Sources about Industries, Corporations, and Finances

Three categories of specific information sources are identified in this chapter: industries information, corporate directory information, and investments/financial/economic information.

INDUSTRIES INFORMATION

Many sources can be used to obtain information about industries. Some are presented in other chapters of Part 2. For example, an important source of secondary data about industries is provided in the federal government's census material. Especially relevant to sources about industries is the government material utilizing the SIC codes. Additional sources identified elsewhere in this book include the *Encyclopedia of Associations* (Chapter 6), *Statistical Reference Index* (Chapter 9), *Encyclopedia of Business Information Sources* (Chapter 10), the *Predicasts Basebook* (Chapter 11), and *Predicasts Forecasts* (Chapter 11). In addition, *The Wall Street Journal* regularly publishes lengthy industry articles complete with extensive tables and graphs. They can be identified through either *The Wall Street Journal Index* (available at libraries) or through *JournalFinder* (an informational product of the Dow Jones News Service, telephone: 800-445-9454).

To identify the numerous published business and industrial

directories, buyers' guides, and rosters (as well as directories of companies located in a particular country, state, or city), the reader is encouraged to consult a guide such as those listed below.

City and State Directories in Print

As its title expresses, this book provides an extensive listing of city and state directories.

Updates: The reader is referred to the latest edition of this book. Updates are published regularly.

Publisher: Gale Research Company (Detroit, MI).

Directories in Print

Provides information about directories, including commercial, manufacturing, industries, trades, professions, professional associations, and scientific societies. The information is organized according to subject and other headings.

Updates: The reader is referred to the latest edition of this book. Updates are published regularly. The sixth edition was published in 1989.

Publisher: Gale Research Company (Detroit, MI).

FINDEX: The Directory of Market Research Reports, Studies and Surveys

Provides a brief description (but not a summary of findings) for over 11,000 marketing research studies done by more than 500 research firms. It includes citations of market research reports, consumer and product studies, store audit reports, subscription research services, multiclient industry studies, and surveys of fifty-five industries worldwide. For products or topics of interest, the names of related studies, organizations who conducted the studies, contact information, and order procedures for obtaining copies of particular studies are provided. This publication corresponds with the company's on-line data base titled: *FIND/SVP Reports and Studies*

Index (which is described in Chapter 7).

Updates: Annually, with semiannual supplements.

Publisher: Cambridge Information Group Directories (Bethesda, MD).

International Directories in Print

Provides a listing of about 5,000 business directories published outside the United States.

Updates: The reader is referred to the latest edition of this book. Updates are published regularly.

Publisher: Gale Research Company (Detroit, MI).

Predicasts F&S Index United States

Provides information about companies (including mergers and acquisitions), products (including new developments), and industries (including developments in technology). The information is organized according to company name, SIC number, and company according to SIC categories. This information is obtained from more than 750 sources such as brokerage house reports, business newspapers and magazines, trade magazines, and various financial publications.

This index has a unique feature. It provides information that identifies current articles and portions of articles which pertain to news, financial data, and marketing information about United States companies.

There are also two analogous data bases published by Predicasts that do not focus on the United States. These are Predicasts F&S Index Europe (which focuses on Europe) and Predicasts F&S Index International (which focuses on countries in the world other than Europe and the United States). All three of these sources are also available on the on-line data base, PTS F&S Index.

Updates: Weekly (with monthly, quarterly, and annual culminations.

Publisher: Predicasts, Inc. (Cleveland, OH).

PTS PROMPT

The acronym stands for "Predicasts Overview of Markets and Technology." PTS PROMPT is also available as an on-line data base, as well as CD-ROM. For complete discussion of this secondary data source, the reader is referred to the more complete discussion of the *PTS PROMPT* data base (in Chapter 7).

Updates: Monthly (with quarterly and annual culminations).
Publisher: Predicasts, Inc. (Cleveland, OH).

Standard & Poor's Industry Surveys

Provides "Basic Analysis" surveys for each of about thirty industries in the United States. Included in this information are comparative statistics for leading companies in the respective industry. These basic analysis surveys are supplemented by three shorter publications (*Current Analysis*), which are issued three times a year with correspondingly more current data.

Updates: Annually (supplement by three updates during the year).
Publisher: The Standard & Poor's Corporation (New York).

U.S. Industrial Outlook

Provides brief discussions of recent trends on each of approximately 350 manufacturing and service industries. Included in this information are expected prospects for the next five years.

Updates: Annually
Publisher: United States International Trade Administration of the Department of Commerce (Washington, DC).

CORPORATE DIRECTORY INFORMATION

This section identifies several major, long-established directories of corporations. While not usually of value to most people who perform marketing research projects, there may be the occasional project to which they are invaluable.

There are many more directories and guides both in general and in particular to specific countries, states, and cities. The directories especially helpful in identifying such guides is the *Directories in Print* published by Gale Research Company (Detroit, Michigan) and the *City and State Directories in Print*, also published by the Gale Research Company. A third such publication by the Gale Research Company has worldwide coverage and is titled *International Directories in Print*. This publication lists over five thousand directories published outside the United States.

Advertising Age

In special issues of *Advertising Age*, such agency information as total billings, billings according to media, accounts won and lost, and gross income are provided in the two following descriptively titled issues, (1) *U.S. Advertising Agency Profiles* (updated annually in March), and (2) *Foreign Agency Income Reports* (updated annually in April, with information arranged according to country).

In another special issue, such advertiser information as advertising budget/expenditures, sales, profits, product lines and brands, market share, and advertising personnel are provided in the descriptively titled, *100 Leading National Advertisers* (updated annually in September).

Two additional special issues are also (1) the *Top 100 Leading Markets* (updated every three years) and (2) the *100 Leading Media Companies* (updated annually in June).

Publisher: Crain Communications (Chicago, IL).

Broadcasting

In addition to the regular magazine issues, *Broadcasting* publishes a special issue titled *Broadcasting Cablecasting Yearbook*. This yearbook provides directory information of television and radio stations located in the United States and Canada, and respective household information in regard to the stations. Information is provided for both broadcast television stations and cable television systems.

Updates: Annually, each spring.
Publisher: Broadcasting Publications (Washington, DC).

Directory of Corporate Affiliations

Provides information on more than 4,000 parent companies in the United States and their approximately 50,000 subsidiaries, divisions, and affiliates. The information is organized according to SIC code, state, and alphabetical order. Included in this information is a listing of mergers, acquisitions, and names changes that have occurred since 1976.
Updates: Annually.
Publisher: National Register Publishing Company (Wilmette, IL).

Dun's Market Identifiers

For a complete discussion of this secondary data source, the reader is referred to the more complete discussion of the D&B Dun's Market Identifiers data base within Chapter 7.

The Fortune 500

Provides a listing of the 500 largest industrial corporations in the United States. These companies are ranked by sales, assets, profits, and so forth, and are categorized according to industry.
Updates: Annually (as part of a second issue in April of *Fortune* magazine).
Publisher: Time, Inc. (New York).

The Fortune International 500

Provides a listing of the 500 largest industrial corporations and the 100 largest commercial banks located outside the United States. Also included is a listing of the 100 largest companies in the world (regardless of location).

Updates: Annually (as part of the second issue in July, of *Fortune* magazine).

Publisher: Time, Inc. (New York).

The Fortune Service 500

Provides separate listings of companies located in the United States according to the following categories: diversified service companies (100 largest), commercial banks (100 largest), diversified financial companies (50 largest), life insurance companies (50 largest), retailers (50 largest), transportation companies (50 largest), and utilities (50 largest).

Updates: Annually (as part of the first issue in June, of *Fortune* magazine).

Publisher: Time, Inc. (New York).

Greenbook: International Directory of Marketing Research Companies and Services

Provides a descriptive listing of marketing research companies in the United States and in other countries. While these companies are listed alphabetically, there is also an index by geographic location, as well as numerous other indexes.

Updates: Annually.

Publisher: New York Section of the American Marketing Association (New York).

How to Find Information about Companies: The Corporate Intelligence Source Book

Provides information about locating information regarding particular companies.

Updates: Published in 1988 in its sixth edition; the reader is referred to the latest edition available.

Publisher: Washington Researchers (Washington, DC).

International Directory of Corporate Affiliations

Similar to the *Directory of Corporate Affiliations* by the same publisher, this *International Directory of Corporate Affiliations* provides information about parent companies and their subsidiaries, divisions, and affiliates. This information includes holdings in the United States by foreign parent companies and holdings outside of the United States by domestic companies.

Updates: Annually.

Publisher: National Register Publishing Company (Wilmette, IL).

Journal of Advertising Research

Provides information specifically of interest to advertising, including the results of scholarly research projects, literature reviews, and various other marketing communications information.

Updates: Bimonthly.

Publisher: Advertising Research Foundation (New York).

Million Dollar Directory

Provides brief information concerning about 160,000 public or private businesses in the United States whose worth is more than $1 million. Information provided includes officers/directors, approximate sales, number of employees, stock exchange ticker symbol, and SIC code numbers. Companies are categorized according to geographic location and SIC industry. *A separate publication, titled the Top 50,000 Companies*, presents only the largest of these 160,000 businesses.

Updates: Annually.

Publisher: Cooperatively by Dun and Bradstreet (New York) and Dun's Marketing Services (Parsippany, NJ). Available in printed book form, as an on-line data base, and in CD-ROM format.

Standard & Poor's Register of Corporations Directors, and Executives

Provides information about officers, products, sales, addresses, telephone numbers, and employees for over 50,000 companies in the United States and Canada. This publication is similar to the *Million Dollar Directory*. It is therefore a valuable source to cross-check the accuracy of information. Furthermore, because this *Standard & Poor's Register* is not identical to the *Million Dollar Directory*, it is a valuable complement which provides similar but different information. For example, part of the *Standard & Poor's Register* includes additional brief facts about the company's officers and directors.

Updates: Annually (with intermittent supplements).

Publisher: The Standard & Poor's Corporation (New York). Available in printed book form, as an on-line data base and in CD-ROM format.

Standard Directory of Advertisers

Provides information on more than 25,000 companies in the United States, each with annual advertising expenditures of more than $75,000. Of special interest to marketing researchers, this publication includes names of marketing and sales personnel, as well as the specific advertising agency used by specific advertisers. Also included is information about products advertised, media used, and advertising budgets. This directory is published in two volumes: a *Geographic Index* and a *Trade Name Index/Standard Industrial Classification Index*.

Updates: Annually (with intermittent supplements).

Publisher: National Register Publishing Company (Wilmette, IL).

Standard Directory of Advertising Agencies

Provides information that supplements, or rather complements, the material presented in the *Standard Directory of Advertisers*. This information provides the approximate annual billings for each of about 5,000 advertising agency located in the United States, and the names

of accounts for each agency.
   Updates: Three times per year.
   Publisher: National Register Publishing Company (Wilmette, IL).

Standard Directory of Worldwide Marketing

Provides information similar to that described in regard to the *Standard Directory of Advertisers*. The major difference is that this directory provides information about companies outside the United States and correspondingly includes the names of related advertising agencies located outside the United States.
   Updates: Annually.
   Publisher: National Register Publishing Company (Wilmette, IL).

Television and Cable Factbook

Provides information similar to that provided by the special *Broadcasting* issue titled *Broadcasting Cablecasting Yearbook*.
   Updates: Annually.
   Publisher: Television Digest, Inc. (Washington, DC).

Thomas Register of American Manufacturers

Provides information on manufacturing firms in the United States: addresses, products produced, approximate assets, branch offices, and subsidiaries. Within this information there are more than 145,000 companies listed according to product, brand name, and alphabetical order. The various volumes are ordered as follows: indexes to manufacturers by product (Volumes 1-7), list of trade names (Volume 7), manufacturers by company name (Volume 8), and a collection of manufacturers' catalogues (Volumes 9-12). There is a catalog file (Volumes 15-21: *Thomas Register Catalog File*) and information similar to that presented in *Standard and Poor's Register* (Volume 8).
   It might be noted that the *Thomas Register of American Manufacturers* is a valuable tool for marketing researchers who need to identify either a particular American manufacturing company or to

identify who manufactures a particular brand.

Updates: Annually.

Publisher: Thomas Publishing Company (New York), in twenty-one volumes. All are available in printed book form, as an on-line data base (Thomas Register On-line) and in CD-ROM format.

INVESTMENTS/FINANCIAL/ECONOMIC INFORMATION

This section identifies secondary data sources that pertain most directly to financial considerations. These sources heavily emphasize the investment and financial aspects of companies.

Almanac of Business and Industrial Financial Ratios

Provides information about the number of establishments, their assets, their sales and various operating ratios for various industries. This information permits comparative analysis of a particular company's financial ratios with their competitors. The data are obtained from tax return information provided by the U.S. Internal Revenue Service.

Updates: Annually.

Publisher: Prentice-Hall (Englewood Cliffs, NJ).

Commodity Year Book

Provides statistics on prices, production, exports, stocks, and so forth for about one hundred commodities.

Updates: Annually.

Publisher: Commodity Research Bureau (New York).

Corporate Annual Reports

These sources of secondary data are reports that companies issue to their stockholders, investment brokerage firms, and other interested parties. Normally they are in printed form, but libraries regularly also have them in microfiche form. Some companies also have a videotaped version. All these formats are readily available at either libraries (especially university libraries) or directly from the company of interest via a written or telephone request. Corporate annual reports exist for all "publicly held" companies in the United States. Similar reports are also available for many companies located outside the United States. Corporate annual reports are often the product of very sophisticated departments of public relations and production and printing facilities. Consequently, their information, albeit accurate, must be utilized cautiously for an exaggerated slant.

Updates: Annually.

Publisher: Specific company.

Economic Indicators

Provides data on topics that indicate the country's economic condition: prices, wages, money, credit, gross national product, personal consumption, federal finance, production, etc. Some of these statistics date back to 1939.

Updates: Monthly.

Publisher: U.S. Council of Economic Advisors (Washington, DC).

Economic Report of the President

This report is comprised primarily of two sections. The first section reflects the American president's annual address to Congress, which discusses the economic well-being of the United States. The second section is the annual report of the U.S. Council of Economic Advisors, in which statistics relating to income, employment, and production, are presented.

Updates: Annually.

Publisher: U.S. Government Printing Office (Washington, DC).

Federal Reserve Bulletin

Provides financial and economic statistics, such as interest rates, savings rates, industrial production, banking, loans, investments, securities prices, fund flows, money market data, and international trade data.

Updates: Monthly.

Publisher: Board of Governors of the U.S. Federal Reserve System (Washington, DC).

Investext

On-line data base that provides full-text coverage of financial research reports. These reports are about companies and industries prepared by financial analysts at over fifty investment banking firms and other financial research firms. While these investment and financial firms are primarily in the United States, the information is global. Furthermore, information is also provided from financial analysts conducted in firms located in Canada, Europe, and Japan.

Moody's Handbook of Common Stocks

Provides brief, current financial statistics on each of over 900 listed stocks. These stocks reflect those with relatively high investor interest. A similar publication (also updated quarterly) is *Moody's Handbook of OTC Stocks* for stocks with high investor interest and traded Over The Counter.

Updates: Quarterly.

Publisher: Moody's Investors Service (New York).

Moody's Manuals

Provides information pertaining to finances of individual companies and various government agencies. Actual information varies somewhat according to company, but for each company for which full information is presented, there is typically a brief financial history, nature of the business and its products, subsidiaries, officers and directors, letter to stockholders from the chief executive officer, seven years of income and balance sheet data, and financial and operating data. The respective manuals are descriptively titled, as follows:

Moody's Industrial Manual provides financial information about industrial corporations traded on the New York Stock Exchange, the American Stock Exchange, and regional stock exchanges.

Moody's Over The Counter Industrial Manual provides financial information about industrial companies traded over the counter (OTC).

Moody's Bank and Finance Manual (four volumes).

Moody's International Manual (two volumes).

Moody's Municipal & Government Manual (three volumes).

Moody's OTC Unlisted Manual.

Moody's Public Utility Manual (two volumes).

Moody's Transportation Manual.

Updates: Annually (with some weekly supplements).
Publisher: Moody's Investors Service (New York) in a series of eight different manuals. Each manual is available in printed form, on-line data base, and CD-ROM format.

Nelson's Directory of Investment Research

Provides information for identifying investment analysts who focus on a particular company. Included in this information is a listing of companies around the world, complete with the names of corresponding analysts and the names of their respective investments firms. This directory includes a short list of financial research reports on particular companies during the previous year. Furthermore, there are numerous indexes such as one that lists analysts by industry and another that lists companies by geographic location. A related supplement to the *Nelson's Directory of Investment Research* is a separate publication titled *Nelson's Global Research*. The latter is published ten times a year and provides lists of the current year's research reports.
Updates: Annually.
Publisher: Nelson Publications (Port Chester, NY).

Predicasts F&S Index United States

This secondary data base is discussed in detail in Chapter 10. Therefore, the reader is referred to that more complete discussion titled *Predicasts F&S Index United States*.

Updates: Annually (with monthly, quarterly, and annual culminations).

Publisher: Predicasts, Inc. (Cleveland, OH).

Quarterly Financial Report (QFR)

Provides financial statistics for manufacturing industries, as obtained from American corporation income statements, balance sheets, and various financial operating ratios. Also included is more limited, but similar, information pertaining to companies in the mining, wholesale, and retail industries.

Updates: Quarterly.

Publisher: U.S. Bureau of the Census (Washington, DC) and formerly by the U.S. Federal Trade Commission.

Standard & Poor's Corporate Records

Provides historical (since 1925) and current information. As well as financial information, this information includes corporate news, company history, officers, and product information. This information pertains to companies in the United States, Canada, and other parts of the world. A related publication, *Daily News*, provides more current related developments.

Updates: Semimonthly.

Publisher: Standard & Poor's Corporation (New York). Available in printed, looseleaf format.

Standard & Poor's Statistical Service

Provides historical and current data (business and economic), reported within sections designated as banking and finance; production indexes and labor statistics; price indexes (commodities producer and consumer price indexes, cost of living); income and trade; building and building materials; electric power and fuels; metals; transportation; textiles, chemicals, paper; agricultural products; Security Price Index Record. Also included are long-term trends for Standard & Poor's stock price index and Dow Jones averages.

Updates: Monthly.

Publisher: Standard & Poor's Corporation (New York). Available in printed, looseleaf format.

Standard Corporation Descriptions

Information is similar to that provided in the Moody's Manuals. The primary difference is that information is arranged alphabetically by company. In contrast, the Moody's Manuals arrange information according to type of operation (e.g., transportation, utilities, etc.)

Updates: Monthly (with semimonthly supplements). Moreover, there are some daily updates in the form of the company's *Current News Edition.*

Publisher: The Standard & Poor's Corporation (New York). Available in printed, looseleaf format (six volumes), as an on-line data base (Standard & Poor's Corporation Descriptions On-line), and in CD-ROM format.

Standard NYSE Stock Reports

Provides information about companies listed on the New York Stock Exchange (NYSE). The information includes a concise summary of the nature of the business, important recent developments, current income and balance sheet figures, revenue per share, and dividend and other data. Similar information is also provided by this company for companies whose stocks are listed on the American Stock Exchange and are traded over the counter.

Updates: Every three months (with irregular, intermittent supplements).

Publisher: The Standard & Poor's Corporation (New York).

Available in printed, looseleaf format (four volumes, with supplemental pages provided).

Statistics of Income

Provides information about income collected by the U.S. Internal Revenue Service. This information is presented in two volumes: one pertaining to individual tax returns and the other pertaining to corporations. The corporation volume includes tables arranged by industry and asset size.

Updates: Annually. In addition, there is a related bulletin that is updated quarterly (*SOI Bulletin*), which provides information on income in terms of individuals, partnerships, sole proprietorships, and corporations.

Publisher: U.S. Internal Revenue Service of the American Treasury Department (Washington, DC).

Survey of Current Business

As an important source for current business statistics, this source is especially known for its data on national income, gross national product, personal consumption expenditures, international transactions, and foreign direct investments in the United States In addition, it contains data pertaining to general business indicators, commodity prices, employment and earnings, domestic trade, finance, foreign trade, and major manufacturing industries.

Updates: Monthly.

Publisher: U.S. Bureau of Economic Analysis (Washington, DC).

10-K Reports

These sources of secondary data are reports that "publicly held" companies must file annually with the Securities and Exchange Commission of the U.S. government. Normally, they are in printed form, but libraries regularly also have them in microfiche form. This information is available at libraries (especially university libraries), investment brokerage firms, and/or directly from the company of interest via a written or telephone request. Because this government requires certain information about the company's operations, the 10-K reports of company might provide different (and more trustworthy) information then that provided in a corresponding corporate annual report.

Updates: Annually.
Publisher: Specific company.

Value Line Investment Survey

Provides information in three parts: (1) an index and summary section, (2) newsletter, and (3) company and industry reports. Included in this information, are one-page statistical profiles of 1,700 companies in about ninety-five industries. The information is arranged in thirteen sections according to industry. Among the information are a fifteen-year table for twenty-three key financial and operating figures, three-year projections, several "Value Line ratings," and a brief outlook. It might be noted that in contrast to publications by Moody's and Standard & Poor's, the Value Line Investment Survey is an investment advisory product.

Updates: Weekly.
Publisher: Value Line, Inc. (New York). Available in printed form (looseleaf), on-line data base (Value Line Data Base-II), and on CD-ROM format.

The Wall Street Journal

Content involves both newspaper articles and financial data. The newspaper is available in print. Its news articles are also available in a full-text on-line data base called the Dow Jones News Services. Its financial data, such as stock prices, bond prices, and financial information, are available in a separate on-line data base called the Dow Jones Quotes.

A related product by the Dow Jones News Services is Facts Delivered. It provides information from the company's many news-wire services and computerized file periodicals. Included are full text articles from *The Wall Street Journal*, *Barrons*, and hundreds of other regional, national, and international business publications. Another product available through the Dow Jones News Services is Journal-Finder. JournalFinder offers reprints or stories from *The Wall Street Journal*, *Barrons*, and the Dow Jones News Service. Still another service is Facts Delivered: Corporate Reports, that provides comprehensive reports on thousands of publicly traded companies. These reports are delivered by fax, e-mail, or traditional mail.

The Wall Street Journal goes beyond financial data and financial stories. Typically it includes three sections. Only the last section (Section C, "Money and Investing") focuses on prices and other financial data for stocks, corporate bonds, government issues, options, futures, mutual fund tables, stock price indexes, and foreign exchange rates. The first section provides somewhat general interest news articles about business, politics, economics, international developments, politics, and other editorial matters. The second section (Section B, "Marketplace") provides articles on topics such as marketing, consumers, advertising, marketing and media, company strategy, technology, and legal issues.

Updates: Daily for *The Wall Street Journal* itself and monthly for *The Wall Street Journal Index*. In addition, there are annual culminations of the index.

Publisher: Dow Jones and Company (New York).

11

General Business
Information Sources

Two categories of secondary data sources are identified in this chapter: business information not specific to marketing, and general and dissimilar information.

BUSINESS INFORMATION
(NOT SPECIFIC TO MARKETING)

The list of indexes identified here are not specific to marketing research or to marketing. However, they include specific business and technology indexes that are important to those who perform marketing research.

ABI/Inform

This is a data base frequently used by people interested in marketing research and marketing, and who are familiar with on-line databases. As well as marketing, topics covered include accounting, finance, management, international trade, law, advertising, banking, human resources, and telecommunications. This on-line data base provides abstracts for articles published in more than 800 business periodicals. The abstracts are searched and located according to subject, author, or key word. A companion data base (BPO for Business Periodicals Ondisk) is a full text system of the articles in about 300 ABI/Inform indexed periodicals.

Updates: Monthly.

Publisher: University Microfilms (Ann Arbor, MI).

Available as an on-line data base through vendors such as BRS, DIALOG, ORBIT, and NEXIS, and in CD-ROM format.

American Business Information, Inc.

This is a data base that provides information on more than nine million businesses. Desired businesses can be identified by company name, geographic location, number of employees, sales volume, or by SIC Code.

Publisher: American Business Information, Inc., Optical Products Division (Omaha, NE).

Available on CD-ROM, and is compatible to download to an IBM or IBM-clone personal computer.

Business Information: How to Find It, How to Use It

Provides information for locating business information.

Updates: The reader is referred to the latest edition of this book. It was published in its first edition in 1987.

Publisher: Oryx Press (Phoenix, AZ).

Business Periodicals Index

This is a data base frequently used by people interested in marketing research and marketing. Its popularity is influenced by its familiarity, since the printed version by the same name has been a long-stay of business, and marketing, research; as well as one of the first business indexes to which university students were traditionally exposed early in their college education. Its focus is to provide information about articles that are published in more than 300 American business periodicals. To a lesser extent, it provides information on articles in a relatively few academic or scholarly journals and a relatively few business periodicals published outside the United States. Also provided is an index of business book reviews.

Updates: Monthly (with quarterly and annual culminations).

Publisher: H. W. Wilson Company (New York). Available as both an on-line data base (WILSONLINE) and in CD-ROM format.

Business Statistics

Provides information about the monthly *Survey of Current Business*. Information includes extensive historical tables, including explanatory notes that describe the tables and states the original sources for the data.

Updates: Every two years.

Publisher: U.S. Department of Commerce.

Consultants and Consulting Organizations Directory

Provides information that lists over 14,000 individuals and firms that provide consulting services. This information is organized according to their services, fields of interest, location, and name.

Updates: The reader is referred to the latest edition of this book. Updates are published regularly. It was published in its ninth edition in 1989.

Publisher: Gale Research (Detroit, MI).

County and City Data Book

Supplements the *Statistical Abstract*. Information includes income, population, education, employment, housing, banking, manufacturing, capital expenditures, mineral and agricultural production, retail sales, wholesale sales, voting records, and more. The data are obtained from government censuses and government publications and are reported according to counties and cities in the United States.

Updates: Every five years.

Publisher: U.S. Department of Commerce.

County Business Patterns

Provides information in relation to SIC codes for every state and county in the United States. Specifically, for every four-digit SIC industry code, data are provided for the respective type of business, number of businesses by employment size, and payroll for the financial, insurance, and real estate industries; which represent important service industries whose data are not reported in the *Census of Retail Trade* or the *Census of Service Industries*.

Updates: Annually.

Publisher: U.S. Bureau of the Census (Washington, DC) and available on-line through CENDATA.

Dow Jones News Service

This on-line data base is promoted, by the Dow Jones Company, as "the lifeblood of business." Both current and historical business information is provided on an up-to-the-second basis. The information is drawn from proprietary newswires, the Dow Jones News Service, the Dow Jones Capital Markets Report, Public Relations Newswire, BusinessWire, the full text of *The Wall Street Journal*, and hundreds of local, regional, and national business publications. Two other information services provided by the Dow Jones Company (and discussed in detail in Chapter 10 under the section designated, *The Wall Street Journal*) are the JournalPhone and JournalFinder.

Updates: Continuously.

Publisher: Dow Jones Information Services.

Dun and Bradstreet's Reference Book of Corporate Management

Provides information in the form of a directory of top level executives at companies in the United States. Information is arranged according to company, birth date, college, and employment history.

Updates: Annually.

Publisher: Dun and Bradstreet (New York).

Harvard Business Review Data Base

On-line data base that is the computer version with full text of the articles that appear in the *Harvard Business Review*.

Available through such vendors as BRS, Dialog, Data-Star, and Mead.

Historical Statistics of the United States: Colonial Times to 1970

Serves as a supplement to the *Statistical Abstract of the United States*. While a marketing researcher must put the data into its proper time perspective, this source of secondary data can provide valuable, long-term, historical data pertaining to many social, economic, and political aspects of life in the United States. Of course, as indicated in the general discussion on secondary data, such data over this span of time presents difficulties in comparison due to changes in definitions and categorizations.

Publisher: U.S. Bureau of the Census (Washington, DC).
Published in two volumes, in 1975.

The Information Catalog

Provides information about business topics. This information includes summaries of directories, articles, and reports produced by the FIND/SVP research firm, other research firms, investment brokerage firms, and various publishers.

Updates: Bimonthly.
Publisher: FIND/SVP (New York).

Management Contents

The information provided is reproductions of the table of contents for about 150 business journals.

Updates: Biweekly.

Publisher: G. D. Searle & Co. (Skokie, IL). Available in print and as an on-line data base.

Monthly Labor Review

Provides information about nationwide labor conditions and trends. Statistics include labor force data (such as employment, unemployment, hours), wages and earnings, collective bargaining, price data (such as consumer and producer price indexes), productivity, injury, and illness.

Updates: Monthly.
Publisher: U.S. Bureau of Labor Statistics (Washington, DC).

Predicasts Basebook

Provides comprehensive statistics in the form of approximately 26,000 time series that involve specific products, specific industries, basic economic indicators, calculated growth rate, and the source for the original statistics. This information is reported according to the seven-digit Standard Industrial Classification (SIC) system.

Updates: Annually.
Publisher: Predicasts, Inc. (Cleveland, OH). Available in printed, looseleaf format and as an on-line data base known as PTS Time Series.

Predicasts Forecasts

Provides both short- and long-range statistical forecasts for products and industries in the United States. These forecasts often include projections about shipments, production, sales, consumption, and exports. The information are reported according to the seven-digit SIC system. Since they are obtained from a host of journal articles, newspapers, government publications, and other sources, the source for data are also reported.

Publisher: Predicasts, Inc. (Cleveland, OH). Available as an on-line data base known as PTS Forecasts.

Public Affairs Information Service Bulletin

Provides a selective index of articles on business, economics, public administration, and other social sciences. Sources are indexed include magazines, books, government publications, and various pamphlets.

Updates: Monthly (with periodic culminations).

Publisher: Public Affairs Information Services (New York). Available in printed form, as an on-line data base (PAIS International) and in CD-ROM format.

Social Indicators

Provides statistics and trends on social conditions: health, public safety, education, employment, income, housing, leisure and recreation, and population. The value of these data are questionable for marketing researchers since there appears to be no recent update.

Publisher: U.S. Bureau of the Census (Washington, DC).

State and Metropolitan Data Book

Supplements the *Statistical Abstract*. Information includes data about population, housing, government, manufacturing, retail and wholesale trade, and services. These data are reported according to state and standard metropolitan statistical areas.

Publisher: U.S. Department of Commerce.

Statistical Abstract of the United States

A particularly valuable statistical reference book for marketing researchers. It provides information about social, political, and economic issues in the form of statistical tables. The data for these tables are obtained from various government reports, and the respective reference citation is provided for those interested in such greater detail. Also included is information about various guides to statistics, state statistical abstracts, and availability of statistics

pertaining to countries other than the United States.
Updates: Annually.
Publisher: U.S. Bureau of the Census (Washington, DC).

The Wall Street Journal Index

Provides information on articles and various news items published in *The Wall Street Journal.* The information is organized according to subject and company. The index is comprised of a general news section and corporate news section.
Updates: Monthly (with annual culminations).
Publisher: Dow Jones Books (Princeton, NJ).

GENERAL AND DISSIMILAR INFORMATION

The sources of secondary data presented in this section represent a mixture. They do not represent less valuable sources, but rather sources of information that are not particular to any specific category. However, it might be noted that in many marketing research projects, these sources are the most valuable because of their specializations.

Applied Science and Technology Index

Provides information about articles in more than 300 journals in highly technological fields. These fields include geology, oceanography, petroleum, gasoline, physics, plastics, engineering, telecommunications, and environmental engineering.
Updates: Monthly (with periodic culminations).
Publisher: H. W. Wilson Company (New York). Available as both an on-line data base (*WILSONLINE*) and in CD-ROM format.

Computer Readable Databases

Provides information pertaining to about seven thousand data bases. This publication is truly an essential source of information to consult when searching for secondary data related to marketing.

Updates: The reader is referred to the latest edition of this publication. Updates are published regularly. It was published in its eighth edition in 1992.

Publisher: Cuadra/Gale (Gale Research, Detroit, MI).

Corporate 500: The Directory of Corporate Philanthropy

Provides information about philanthropy of the 500 largest companies in the United States, including statements about what qualifies for the company's support. The information includes names and addresses of the company headquarters, board members, committee members, contact people, and past grant recipients.

Updates: The reader is referred to the latest edition of this book. It was published in its second edition in 1982.

Publisher: Public Management Institute (Detroit: MI).

Directory of American Research and Technology

Provides information about research and development (R&D) capabilities in more than 11,000 companies in the United States. This information contains the names of organizations, organized according to alphabetical order and fields of specialization. Also included are the addresses and sizes of the organizations.

Updates: The reader is referred to the latest edition of this publication. Updates are published regularly. It was published in its twenty-third edition in 1989.

Publisher: Bowker (New York).

Directory of Online Data Bases

Provides information about more than 5,000 data bases. A truly essential source when beginning to search for secondary data.

Updates: The reader is referred to the latest edition of this publication. Updates are published regularly. It was published in its thirteenth volume in 1992.

Publisher: Cuadra/Gale (Gale Research, Detroit, MI).

Dissertation Abstracts International

Provides information about doctoral dissertations from about 500 educational institutions in the United States and around the world. The information is organized according to three broad categories and many subcategories. The three broad categories are humanities and social sciences, sciences and engineering, and European abstracts.
Updates: Monthly.
Publisher: University Microfilms (Ann Arbor, MI).

Encyclopedia of Associations

Provides information about associations, such as their names and activities. This information is organized into four volumes: *National Organizations of the United States* (Volume 1), *Geographic and Executive Index* (Volume 2), *New Associations and Projects* (Volume 3), and *International Organizations* (Volume 4).
Updates: Annually. The reader is referred to the latest edition.
Publisher: Gale Research Company (Detroit, MI).

Encyclopedia of Information Systems

Provides information about organizations involved in secondary data via computerized storage and retrieval. The information includes names, addresses, and descriptions about data base producers, publishers, vendors, information centers, research centers, and data banks. This publication is supplemented periodically by a publication titled *New Information Systems and Services*.
Updates: Annually. The reader is referred to the latest edition. It was published in its ninth edition in 1989.
Publisher: Gale Research Company (Detroit: MI).

The Federal Register

Provides information about all regulatory affairs pertaining to, and issued by, all agencies and offices of the American federal govern-

ment. The information is official, comprehensive, and indexed.
Updates: Daily.
Publisher: Division of the Federal Register, National Archives (Washington, DC).

Guide to U.S. Government Publications

Provides information in the form of an annotated guide about the publications of government agencies throughout the United States.
Updates: Annually (since 1973).
Publisher: U.S. Government, Document Index (McLean, VA).

Index to Publications of the U.S. Congress

Provides information in the form of indexes and abstracts about the working papers of the United States Congress. This information spans the entire range of congressional publications.
Updates: Quarterly (with annual culminations).
Publisher: U.S. Government (Washington, DC).

Reader's Guide to Periodical Literature

Provides an index of more than 150 general interest magazines in the United States. Periodicals considered to be business, academic, or scholarly are not indexed. Information is searched and located according to subject and author.
Updates: Monthly (with periodic culminations).
Publisher: H. W. Wilson Company (New York). Available in printed form, as an on-line data base (WILSONLINE) and in CD-ROM format.

SilverPlatter

Provides information in index form for more than 350,000 audio-video items (videotapes, 16mm films, audiotapes, slides, transparencies, etc.) that are educational, documentary, or otherwise informational.

Updates: Annually.

Publisher: SilverPlatter International (Boston, MA).

Social Sciences Citation Index

Provides information about articles published in about 1,400 social science periodicals and about 3,500 periodicals in other disciplines.

Updates: Three times a year (with annual culminations).

Publisher: Institute for Scientific Information (Philadelphia, PA).

Concluding Comment

Many specific sources of secondary data exist. There are so many, that dealing with them can be confusing and, even, overwhelming. Moreover, while the number of secondary data sources available is already large, it is increasing every moment. Similarly, the technologies to archive, access, and retrieve these sources are changing.

It is important for individuals who conduct marketing research to be as efficient and effective as possible when locating the desired information. Fortunately, the task is becoming easier, even in the midst of an increasing quantity of available information. The reason is due to computerization. Data bases themselves are becoming increasingly computerized, as are the means for searching them.

Specific secondary data sources are available in different formats. The traditional format of print is still alive and well, but at the same time, increasing amounts of more printed information are being converted to electronic forms. These electronic forms, by and large, represent computer technology with which the marketing researchers of a particular project need not be too concerned. However, the bottom line is that computer technology is making it increasingly easy to locate and access these secondary data. As a result, marketing researchers are, now more than ever, able to locate desired information within specific secondary data sources in an efficient and effective manner.

Address correspondence to:

Gordon L. Patzer, Ph.D.
Dean, School of Business Administration
California State University, Stanislaus
801 West Monte Vista Avenue
Turlock, California 95380

Selected Bibliography

Arthur Andersen Company. *The Arthur Andersen North American Business Sourcebook.* Chicago: Triumph Books, 1994.

Bartos, R. "International Demographic Data?" *Marketing and Research Today*, November 1989, pp. 205-212.

Belohlav, James, and Louis Raho. "Successful Planning in the Management Information Maze." *Managerial Planning*, May-June 1984, pp. 30-37.

Bickert, Jock. *Adventures in Relevance Marketing.* Denver, CO: Briefcase Books, 1991.

Borgman, Christine L., Dineh Moghdam, and Patti K. Corbett. *Effective Online Searching: A Basic Text.* New York: Marcel Dekker, 1984.

Brown, Stephen, and Martin Goslar. "New Information Systems for Marketing Decision Making." *Business*, July-September 1988, pp. 18-24.

Chen, C. C., and S. Schweizer. *Online Bibliographic Searching: A Learning Manual.* New York: Neal-Schumen Publishers, 1981.

Daniells, Lorna M., *Business Information Sources.* 3rd ed. Berkeley, CA: University of California Press, 1993.

Delphos, W. A. *The World Is Your Market.* Washington, DC: Braddock Communications, 1990.

Dern, Daniel P. *The Internet Guide for New Users*. New York: McGraw-Hill, 1994.

Falk, Bennett. *The Internet Roadmap*. Alameda, CA: SYBEX, 1994.

"Information Brokers: New Breed with Access to Secondary Research." *Marketing News*, February 27, 1987, p. 14.

Jacob, Herbert. *Using Published Data: Errors and Remedies*. Beverly Hills, CA: Sage Publications, 1984.

Johnson, H. Webster, Anthony J. Faria, and Ernest L. Maier. *How to Use the Business Library: With Sources of Business Information*. 5th ed. Cincinnati, OH: South-Western, 1984.

Kan, Yue-Sai. *Doing Business in Asia*. New York: International Institute for Learning, 1994. Series of four videotapes with some relevance to using secondary data in marketing research and focusing on Japan, Taiwan, Hong Kong, and South Korea.

Lambert, D. M., H. Marmorstein, and A. Sharma. "Industrial Sales People as a Source of Market Information." *Industrial Marketing Management* 2 (1990): 141-148.

Lavin, Michael R. *Business Information, How to Find It, How to Use It*. 2nd ed. Phoenix, AZ: Oryx Press, 1992.

MacFarlane, I. "Do-It-Yourself Marketing Research." *Management Review*, May 1991, pp. 34-37.

"Marketers Increasing Their Use of Decision Support Systems." *Marketing News*, May 22, 1989, p. 29.

Marlow, Cecilia Ann, ed. *Directories in Print*. 10th ed. Detroit, MI: Gale Research, 1992.

Mayros, Van, and D. Michael Werner. *Information Sourcebook for Marketing and Strategic Planners*. Radnor, PA: Chilton Book Company, 1983.

"More Marketers Are Going On Line for Decision Support." *Marketing News*, November 12, 1990, p. 14.

Mossman, Jennifer, ed. *Acronyms, Initialisms and Abbreviations Dictionary 1994*. 18th ed. Detroit, MI: Gale Research, 1994.

O'Brien, Terrence. "Decision Support Systems." *Marketing Research*, December 1990, pp. 51-55.

Pittenger, Donald B. "Gathering Foreign Demographics Is No Easy Task." *Marketing News*, January 8, 1990, p. 23.

Powell, Tim. "Despite Myths, Secondary Research Is a Valuable Tool." *Marketing News*, September 21, 1991, pp. 28, 33.

Schwartz, Joe. "Databases Deliver the Goods." *American Demographics*, September 1989, p. 24.

Stewart, David W. *Secondary Research: Information Sources and Methods*. Beverly Hills, CA: Sage Publications, 1984.

Union of International Association [Brussels], ed. *Yearbook of International Organizations 1993/94*. New Providence, NJ: K. G. Saur/Reed Reference Publishing Company, 1993.

Way, James, ed. *Encyclopedia of Business Information Sources*. 9th ed. Detroit, MI: Gale Research, 1993.

Index

About the Author

GORDON L. PATZER is Dean of the School of Business Administration, California State University, Stanislaus. He has traveled and taught throughout the world, and has developed marketing strategies for the CBS Television Network and Saatchi and Saatchi, an international advertising agency. Among his many publications is *The Physical Attractiveness Phenomena*.

ISBN 0-89930-961-5

EAN

9 780899 309613

90000>

HARDCOVER BAR CODE